Radicalism
in
Minnesota
1900-1960

Radicalism in Minnesota

1900-1960

A Survey of Selected Sources

20th-Century Radicalism in Minnesota Project
Carl Ross, Project Director

MINNESOTA HISTORICAL SOCIETY PRESS • ST. PAUL

Publication of this book was supported, in part, with funds provided by the June D. Holmquist Publications and Research Fund of the Minnesota Historical Society.

Minnesota Historical Society Press
St. Paul 55102

Manufactured in the United States of America
10 9 8 7 6 5 4 3 2 1

International Standard Book Number 0-87351-307-x

☉ The paper used in this publication meets the minimum require-ments of the American National Standard for Information Sciences—Permanence for Printed Library Materials, ANSI Z39.48-1984.

Library of Congress Cataloging-in-Publication Data

Radicalism in Minnesota, 1900–1960 : a survey of selected sources /
    20th-Century Radicalism in Minnesota Project, Carl Ross, project
    director.
        p. cm.
    Includes index.
    ISBN 0-87351-307-x (alk. paper)
    1. Radicalism—Minnesota—History—20th century—Sources
    —Bibliography. I. Ross, Carl, 1913–   II. 20th-Century
    Radicalism in Minnesota Project.
    Z7165.U6M627 1994
    [HN79.M53R3]
    016.30348'4—dc20   94-20239

Contents

Introduction

This bibliography is a product—and in fact a summary of accomplishments—of the 20th-Century Radicalism in Minnesota Project launched by the Research Department of the Minnesota Historical Society in 1987.[1] The project essentially fulfilled its three major goals: (1) to compile a bibliography of sources in the society's collections and other repositories in the state that relate to left-wing political radicalism in Minnesota; (2) to conduct and transcribe oral history interviews and to identify other documentary materials that might be added to the society's holdings, and (3) to encourage utilization of these resources for research and publication on state, local, regional, and national history.

As intended, most of the bibliographic entries describe materials that are located in the collections of the Minnesota Historical Society. In addition, as a result of the generous cooperation of many project associates, this bibliography also includes descriptions of selected items in the holdings of the University of Minnesota libraries, archives, and special collections in Minneapolis; the University of Minnesota's Immigration History Research Center in St. Paul; and five regional historical centers located on university campuses around the state.

To our knowledge this bibliography is the largest listing ever compiled in Minnesota of personal and institutional records and papers, leaflets, tracts, pamphlets, sundry calls to meetings and other events, political programs and statements, regular and sporadic publications, oral histories, films, photographs, and other materials related to radical activity in the state between 1900 and 1960. This compilation is impressive for both the quantity and the quality of the information it holds. It is, however, a survey of sources and makes no claim to comprehensiveness or to complete consistency of materials examined. It represents the work the project was able to accomplish within a limited time period and with limited funds.

SCOPE OF THE BIBLIOGRAPHY

The primary aim was to include available material originating in the Minnesota radical movement of all ideological and political shadings and to document the left wing of the labor, farm, and farmer-labor movements. From the outset the project assumed that it would be impossible to supply references for Minnesota radicalism without also calling attention to the ethnic origins, influences, cultures, and groups that contributed to it. Thus we sought evidence of radicalism within the broad context of labor, farmer-labor, and ethnic history and in relation to radicalism's interaction with mainstream politics and culture.

The bibliography brings together a wide range of materials relating to politics, culture, organizations, activities, and numerous individuals. Its descriptive entries help to identify issues and ideologies of concern to the radicals. The materials also reflect the mass actions, political campaigns, organizational efforts, and cultural activities that constituted a substantial and broad-based Minnesota radicalism. And they cover the continuing controversy engendered by radicals, the public response to them, and the politics and beliefs of their opponents. The work's greatest strength lies in documenting the years from 1930 to 1945 that were the heyday of Minnesota farmer-laborism. This compilation supplies substantial information on labor history, the Nonpartisan League, and the farmer-labor movement, as well as 19th-century antecedents and, particularly, on the years from 1910 to 1920 that were the formative period of 20th-century radicalism.

Since the public perception of the radicals derives at least as much from red-baiting literature and propaganda as from radical publications, we made an effort to list such materials. This literature often inadvertently documents radicalism. For example, in one printed flier, a scurrilous, racist diatribe against open-housing legislation entitled *Jungle Tom-Toms of Minnesota* (see entry no. 223), there appears a two-page declaration of the Communist party's reasons for supporting the legislation; this party statement has not been found in any other source. The scope of the antiradical material may astonish some. It seems to reflect a subterranean current of racist, anti-Semitic, anti-union sentiment and red-baiting beyond what we might suppose has existed in Minnesota.

There are few aspects of state history, and no communities or regions of the state, to which the information in this bibliography is irrelevant. The evidence, compiled from all parts of the state, testifies to an extraordinary preoccupation in Minnesota life over the whole of this century with the subject of radicalism. It may change how future historians will look at Minnesota's past, whether their inquiries delve into the areas of labor, ethnic, or political history, the study of our culture, or local and community history.

DEFINING 20TH-CENTURY RADICALISM

Defining the subject as radicalism in the 20th century suggests a long-range, retrospective view that radicalism has been, throughout American history, a persistent movement reacting to an ever-changing social and political landscape. A strong argument for this thesis is provided in *The Radicalism of the American Revolution* (1991) by Gordon S. Wood, who demonstrates how the Revolution transformed America from a society dominated by an aristocracy to a popular democracy. Sidney Lens traces this current in American society in *Radicalism in America* (1969), while defining it as a historic struggle against privilege. Paul Buhle includes an extraordinarily detailed account of radicalism in the United States from a Marxist perspective in his book, *Marxism in the United State* (1991). Mary Jo Buhle gives us a vision of radicalism within 19th- and 20th-century women's movements in *Women and American Socialism* (1983). The rise of Minnesota radicalism as it relates to regionalism in conflict with growing national centralization of politics and power is documented by Richard M. Valelly in his *Radicalism in the States* (1989). Research, published and unpublished, on Minnesota history included in Chapter 8 of this bibliography amply discusses radical history from its roots to mid-20th century.

For the most part, the historic characteristics of successive waves of radical dissent have been (1) to energize popular movements for protest, reform, and so-cial change; (2) to offer a basic critique of the status quo, generally from a particular philosophical perspective; and (3) to propose or initiate radical social reforms and a vision of a new society. Radical alternatives and their advocates are catalysts for change within societies otherwise wedded to the status quo or threatened by reaction from the right.

Twentieth-century radicalism in the United States is a continuation of 18th- and 19th-century radicalism and is best defined as the radicalism of the industrial age. The radicalism of our century was molded by the specific social, cultural, and political conditions prevailing in our society, and influenced by philosophical and social theories originating in other parts of the world. Minnesota radicalism, specifically, emerged as a product of unique conditions prevailing in the Midwest, a conclusion well documented in this bibliography.

In the public mind, radicalism during the first half of the 20th century was dominated by various Marxist-oriented movements—Socialism, Communism, Trotskyism—and by syndicalism, especially as exemplified by the Industrial Workers of the World. These movements by no means represent the entirety of what was a much larger current of dissent and pressure for social and political reform and for radical changes in American society. Mass movements have far outstripped the ideologically driven political organizations of the left. Massive strike waves, the CIO organizing campaign, agrarian protests, peace movements, radicalized ethnic societies, and, above all, the civil-rights movement went beyond and expanded the traditional left.

The primarily working-class and Marxist-oriented groups have not held a monopoly on the critique of capitalism and the advocacy of revolutionary change. Socialism, a cooperative commonwealth, industrial democracy—all seen as social ideals to replace capitalism—have had their partisans under the umbrella of various philosophies ranging from communism through left-wing populism and farmer-laborism to Christian theology. In the longer view of the American radical past, all of these have their place, as do the abolitionists, 19th-century women's rights advocates, and many, many others extending back to the Sons of Liberty and the reformist utopianism of Roger Williams.

The paradox in the development of left-wing movements is that the radicalism of one generation so often becomes the orthodoxy of the next. Radical ideologies undergo reinterpretation and change, becoming modified in response to society's challenges, or they slip into irrelevant dogmatism, serve reactionary ends, and, sometimes, disappear.

NEW SOURCES ON RADICALISM

In some specific ways the 20th-Century Radicalism in Minnesota Project and this bibliography have broadened the sources from which labor and radical history can be written. The surveys of collections brought to light significant but little-known materials. For example, information about radical activities among unemployed workers and discontented farmers during the 1930s and 1940s and about radical politics from the early 1920s to the 1940s—both relatively undocumented—is provided in the papers of the governors of Minnesota in the State Archives (see Chapter 4) and the political ephemera now cataloged in the society's Research Center (see Chapter 1). The ephemera collection also reflects the activities of the Minnesota Socialist party in the years 1910 to 1919, as does the survey of the society's and the Immigration History Research Center's newspaper holdings describing more than 60 radical newspapers and the Minnesota labor press (see Chapter 2).

In 1989 the project cosponsored a one-day symposium entitled "Voices of Dissent: The Minnesota Radical Press, 1910-1920," featuring the presentation of papers by six international scholars. Exceptional importance attaches to the subject of the symposium: it represents a review of the ideologies and movements during the formative period of Minnesota radicalism in the 20th century. The symposium program opened with an introductory paper by historian Hyman Berman entitled, "Wilson's War and Lenin's Revolution: The American Century Begins." The six authors and the newspapers they wrote about are John E. Haynes on *New Times;* Odd S. Lovoll on *Gaa Paa;* Susanna Frenkel on *Two Harbors Socialist;* Auvo Kostiainen on *Sosialisti, Teollisuustyöläinen,* and *Industrialisti;* Richard Hudelson on *Labor Leader* and *Truth;* Michael Brook on *Solidaritet, Allarm,* and *Facklan.* Copies of the papers, as well as comment and summary by Nancy Roberts and a transcript of the question-and-answer session, are available to researchers in the MHS Research Center.[2]

Oral history sources have been enriched by the project's extensive new interview recordings and transcriptions and by transcriptions made for the first time of oral history interviews conducted in earlier years (see Chapter 3). A majority of the new interviews provide information on radical political activity, farmer-laborism, and the Democratic-Farmer-Labor party. They also offer insights into the personal lives, motivations, and activities of local Communist and Socialist Workers party members, left-wing farmer-laborites, and trade union-

ists. Labor radicalism and culture, especially such New Deal programs as those in worker education and the arts, are strong aspects of the interviews.

Many interviews contain information on the influence of racial and ethnic identity and culture on Minnesota radicalism. African-American history, specifically the history of blacks in the labor movement, is documented in a number of interviews. In others appears information about Jewish radicalism, Slovene culture and politics, Norwegian activists, and a significant number of Finnish Americans.

The project discovered and the society acquired the personal papers of several notable Minnesota activists and identified, in many instances for the first time, the papers of lesser-known, or forgotten, radicals. New acquisitions include the papers of Sam K. Davis, Douglas Alan Bruce, Carl Ross, Wilbur S. Broms, Clayton A. Videen, Chester Bruvold, Samuel Horowitz, and James M. Youngdale. The Bruvold, Horowitz, and Youngdale papers were cataloged after the bibliography was compiled.

In the society's manuscript collection (see Chapter 4) the papers of Minnesota conservatives, mostly Republicans, are shown to be rich in primary source documents created by the radical movement. The records of the Great Northern Railway and the Northern Pacific Railroad are vast, largely unexplored sources of information on labor, radical, and ethnic history (see no. 528 and 605). The bibliography lists files of specifically Minnesota information on radicals, Communists, the IWW, Socialists, labor strikes, farm unrest, and labor spy reports accumulated by detective agencies for company officials.

New sources on women's history appear in most sections of the bibliography and are identified in the index. The entries lead to extensive information on how the labor movement, Nonpartisan League, and radical political organizations have addressed women's issues and what part women played in these movements. The lives of individual women, also indexed by name, are documented in several collections, especially in the new oral history interviews.

THE PROJECT PAPERS

The records of the 20th-Century Radicalism in Minnesota Project are accessible to researchers in the Minnesota Historical Society Research Center (inquire at the reference desk). They are a part of the Minnesota Historical Society Archives. They include research papers and subject files on various topics, such as the Abraham Lincoln Brigade and names of enlisted Minnesotans (partly from Brandeis University); photocopies of excerpts from the Sam Darcy Papers with the minutes of the 1938 Minnesota Communist Party Convention (from Tamiment Institute); and extensive photocopies of Minnesota material from the Socialist Labor Party Collection in the State Historical Society of Wisconsin.

Detailed information gathered by project workers for the collections surveys is available in the following reports, which can be found at the reference desk in the Research Center:

1. "The Radical Press in Minnesota, 1900-1960: A Preliminary Survey of Minnesota Historical Society Holdings," by Elizabeth Raasch-Gilman and Matthew Mulcahy.

2. "Annotated Survey of Holdings on 20th-Century Radicalism in Minnesota in the Minnesota Historical Society Division of Archives and Manuscripts," by Karen Wilson.

3. "A Survey of the Minnesota State Archives: A Listing of Radical/Labor/Farm Movement Materials in the Minnesota Governors' Papers, 1931-1942," by Jerry Flower.

4. "A Survey of Minnesota Labor Materials in the Papers of the Great Northern Railway and Northern Pacific Railroad Companies in the Minnesota Historical Society," by Karen Wilson and John Wickre.

ORGANIZATION OF THE BIBLIOGRAPHY

The bibliography is organized into nine chapters, each a guide to a specific type of material. It begins with Pamphlets and Ephemera, followed by Newspapers; Oral Histories; Archival and Manuscript Collections; Sound and Visual Collection; Artifacts; Periodicals; Books, Unpublished Papers, and Articles; and Selected Works on National and International Radical Activity.

Each section opens with information helpful in gaining access to the items described in the entries that follow. Researchers will be informed about computerized catalogs, supplemental finding aids, and the specific locations of the works included. A listing of all abbreviations used to identify the repositories that are cited in the bibliography appears on page xiv. This list also provides the mailing address for each repository. An explanation of the abbreviations that appear in the descriptive text of many entries is on page xiv. A detailed index completes the bibliography. Its entries refer both to numbered entries (in roman type) and to page numbers (in italic type).

CARL ROSS
Project Director

NOTES

[1] For a report on the 20th-Century Radicalism Project, see entry no. 871 of this bibliography.

[2] Cosponsors for the symposium were the Minnesota Historical Society, the First Unitarian Society of Minneapolis, the Norwegian-American Historical Association, and, from the University of Minnesota, the Immigration History Research Center, the Department of History, the Scandinavian Studies Department, and the Silha Center for the Study of Journalism. The symposium was made possible with the assistance of the Minnesota Humanities Commission, the National Endowment for the Humanities, and the Minnesota State Legislature.

Acknowledgments

The 20th-Century Radicalism in Minnesota Project owes a great deal to many people. In the beginning, the idea of such a project met strong support from Russell W. Fridley, then director of the Minnesota Historical Society, and from Jean A. Brookins, assistant director for publications and research. In 1986 the Society's Research Department awarded me a grant that supported the research and planning necessary to launch the project in 1987. Throughout its duration, the project worked under the guidance and enthusiastic support of Deborah L. Miller, research supervisor, and Jean Brookins.

Compilation of this bibliography required hundreds of hours of work over a period of two years by a small staff, interns, and volunteers and the unstinting cooperation from the MHS Research Department, library and archival staff, and university libraries staff. Sal Salerno, research associate, began the project's bibliographic work; Elizabeth Raasch-Gilman, research associate, later assumed the overall responsibility for coordinating and supervising this aspect of the project.

The project's Steering Committee was an overseeing body that offered guidance throughout the project. The members were Hyman Berman, University of Minnesota; Patrick Coleman, Minnesota Historical Society; Lionel B. Davis, Minneapolis; Russell Fridley; Rhoda R. Gilman, Minnesota Historical Society; Nellie Stone Johnson, Minneapolis; Deborah Miller; Peter J. Rachleff, Macalester College; and Carl Ross.

The MHS Advisory Committee of Richard Cameron, F. Hampton Smith, Patrick Coleman, James E. Fogerty, Deborah Miller, and Bonnie Wilson was a mechanism for initiating and following through on collecting personal and organizational papers, artifacts, printed materials, and photographs.

At various periods of time during the project Sal Salerno, Elizabeth Raasch-Gilman, Catherine Petroski, Susan Douglass, Karen Wilson, and Virginia Hyvärinen were paid members of the project staff. Barbara Tilsen ably transcribed oral history interviews. The project also benefited from research help from volunteers and interns. Among them were Jerry Flower, Susan Bernick, David Skeie, Georg Leidenberger, Nat Hong, John Wickre, Susanna Frenkel, and Matthew Mulcahy.

Many colleagues at other institutions in the state cooperated in supplying information for this bibliography. At the University of Minnesota libraries Carol A. Johnson, William R. La Bissoniere, Dianne C. Legg, Barbara L. Walden, and Julia F. Wallace lent their help. Joel F. Wurl and Timo R. Riippa at the Immigration History Research Center assisted. Penelope J. Krosch, University of Minnesota Archives, provided help with university materials. Patricia K. Maus, Northeast Regional History Center at the University of Minnesota—Duluth, helped with northern Minnesota materials.

At the Minnesota Historical Society many staff members answered numerous questions and cooperated in bringing this project to fruition. They include Faustino Avaloz, Brigid Shields, Patricia Harpole, Alissa Rosenberg, Barbara Jones, and the late Wiley Pope of the Reference Department in the Library and Archives Division and Sherri Gebert Fuller and Peter Latner of the Museum Collections Department in the Museums Division. In the Publications and Research Division Jennifer Delton organized bibliographic materials, Sarah P. Rubinstein edited the manuscript for the MHS Press, Deborah Swanson assisted with the manuscript and photographs, Gloria Haider prepared the manuscript for typesetting, and Sandy Batalden answered research questions during her internship at the MHS Press.

The project also had the benefit of the interested assistance of a number of project associates. They included Hyman Berman, who ably chaired the group; Frank Adams, Minneapolis; Martin Blatt, Massachusetts Office of Labor; Dick Blin, *Duluth Labor World;* Paul Buhle, Providence, R.I.; Clarke A. Chambers, University of Minnesota; Carl H. Chrislock, Augsburg College; Roland Dille, Moorhead State University; George Dizard, Duluth; Susanna Frenkel, Bemidji; Archie

ACKNOWLEDGMENTS

Green, San Francisco; James Green, University of Massachusetts at Boston; John E. Haynes, Library of Congress; Virginia Hyvärinen; Michael G. Karni, Minneapolis; Peter Kivisto, Augustana College, Illinois; Helen Kruth, Minneapolis; Odd S. Lovoll, St. Olaf College; Fred E. Lukermann, University of Minnesota; Patricia Maus; Dana Miller and Ed Nelson, Iron Range Research Center, Chisholm; David L. Nass, Southwest State University, Marshall; Alan Netland, AFSCME Council 96, Duluth; Tom O'Connell, Metropolitan State University, St. Paul; William C. Pratt, University of Nebraska at Omaha; Peter Rachleff; David Riehle, Minneapolis; Neala Schleuning, Mankato State University; Leata Wigg Pearson and Glenn E. Pearson, Duluth; Mary Pruitt, Minneapolis Community College; Linda Schloff, Jewish Historical Society of the Upper Midwest, St. Paul; Kenneth Smemo, Moorhead State University; Sidney Steinberg, West Palm Beach, Fla.; Rudolph J. Vecoli, Immigration History Research Center; K. Marianne Wargelin-Brown, Anoka-Ramsey Community College; James M. Youngdale, Minneapolis; and Steven C. Trimble, Minnesota House of Representatives.

Radicalism
in
Minnesota
1900-1960

REPOSITORIES AND ABBREVIATIONS

Research Center
Minnesota Historical Society (MHS)
345 Kellogg Boulevard West
St. Paul, Minn. 55102

University Archives (Uarch)
Walter Library
University of Minnesota
117 Pleasant St. S.E.
Minneapolis, Minn. 55455

Wilson Library
University of Minnesota
309 19th Ave. S.
Minneapolis, Minn. 55455

Immigration History Research Center (IHRC)
826 Berry St.
St. Paul, Minn. 55114

Northeast Minnesota Historical Center (Duluth)
University of Minnesota–Duluth
Duluth, Minn. 55812

Northwest Minnesota Historical Center (Moorhead)
Moorhead State University
Moorhead, Minn. 56560

Southern Minnesota Historical Center (OMankato)
Mankato State University
Mankato, Minn. 56001

Southwest Minnesota Historical Center (Marshall)
Southwest State University
Marshall, Minn. 56258

West Central Minnesota Historical Center (Rwest central)
University of Minnesota–Morris
Morris, Minn. 56267

AFL   American Federation of Labor
CIO   Congress of Industrial Organizations
DFL   Democratic-Farmer-Labor
F-L   Farmer-Labor
F-LP   Farmer-Labor party
IWW   Industrial Workers of the World
NPL   Nonpartisan League
WPA   Works Progress Administration

Pamphlets and Ephemera

Pamphlets and ephemera are listed below chronologically by date of publication, beginning in 1900. Items that are not identified by collection or location are in the Minnesota Historical Society collections at the Research Center. Items located in the collections of the University of Minnesota Archives (Uarch), the Northeast Minnesota Historical Center in Duluth (Duluth), and the Tell G. Dahllöf Collection of Swedish-Americana at the University of Minnesota (Dahl) are clearly identified.

Most of the items in the Research Center are accessible through the computerized catalog. A substantial number of the ephemera items, however, cannot be found by searching for the author or title in the catalog. These items have been collectively cataloged and can be retrieved under the title, "Minnesota Radicalism Pamphlet Collection." In the bibliography entries, these items are noted as "Mnradpam."

Researchers may find additional posters, fliers, handbills, and similar items in the Society's Manuscripts Collection, State Archives, Sound and Visual Collection, and Museum Collection. Please consult with the curatorial staff members for each collection.

1900

1. Mattson, John. *Samhallet: en Studie Ofver Vart Samhalle Sadant det ar och Sadant det Borde Vara: Eller, Hvilket Parti Bora vi Rosta For? En vigtig Frada for Arbetaren att Ratt Bbesvara*. Minneapolis: Forfattarens Forlag, Forord, 1900. 93 p. In Swedish.

2. Minnesota Social Democratic Party. *Minnesota Social Democratic Bulletin*. Minneapolis, 1900–? On microfilm.

Campaign circular in form of newspaper carried party news and platform.

1902

3. Socialist Party of Minnesota. *The Laborer*. Minneapolis, 1902. On microfilm.

Campaign circular in newspaper form. Carried profiles of Socialist candidates and platform.

1904

4. Engels, Friedrich. *Socialismens Utveckling Fran Utopi till Vetenskap*. Minneapolis: Forskaren Pub. Co.'s Forlag, 1904. 57 p. In Swedish.

Translation by Hjalmar Branting of *Die Entwicklung des Sozialismus von der Utopie zur Wissenschaft*.

5. Marx, Karl, and Friedrich Engels. *Det Kommunistiska Manifestet*. Minneapolis: Forskaren Pub. Co.'s Forlag, 1904. 44 p. In Swedish.

Translated by Axel Daniellson.

6. Public Ownership Party. [Newsprint]. Minneapolis, 1904. 4 p.

1905

7. DeLeon, Daniel. *Industriell Unionism: ett Foredrag Hallet . . . I Union Temple, Minneapolis, Minnesota den 10 Juli 1905; med Anledning af Organisationens Ursprungliga Principforklaring*. New York: Skandinavskia Socialistiska Arbetare-Forbundets Forlag, [1905]. 47 p. In Swedish. (Dahl)

8. DeLeon, Daniel. *Inledningen till Konstituionen af Industrial Workers of the World: ett Foredrag Hallet . . . i Union Temple, Minneapolis, Minnesota den 10 Juli 1905*. New York: Skandinaviska Socialistiska Artbetare-Forbundets Forlag, 1905. 47 p. In Swedish. (Dahl)

9. *Kampen For Tillvaron och Socialismen: Ett Vederlagga Socialismen.* Minneapolis: Forskaren Pub. Co.'s Forlag, 1905. 44 p. In Swedish.
    Answer to Dodel's *Moses oder Darwin?*

10. Skjegstad, Inge. *Det Gaar Fremad: Eller, Socialismen Kommer.* Lengby, Minn., 1905. 40 p. In Swedish.

1906

11. Bang, Gustav. *Den Urkristna Kommunismen.* Minneapolis: Forskaren Pub. Co.'s Forlag, 1906. 29 p. In Swedish.

12. Bergman, Johan. *Slafveriet i Antiken: Ett Blad ur Arbetarklassens Historia.* Minneapolis: Forskaren Pub. Co., 1906. In Swedish. (Dahl)

13. Bracke, Wilhelm. *Ned med Socialisterna?* Minneapolis: Forskaren Pub. Co.'s Forlag, 1906. 30 p. In Swedish.
    Translation of *Nieder mit den Sozialdemokraten!*

1908

14. Aley, H. S. *Socialism och Evolution.* Translated by Ernest A. Spongberg. Minneapolis: Forskaren Pub. Co.'s Forlag, 1908. 15 p. In Swedish.

1909

15. Bang, Gustav. *Anarkismen.* Minneapolis: Forskaren Pub. Co.'s Forlag, 1909. 20 p. In Swedish.

1912

16. Enge, Algot. *Ett Genmale till Pastor John Johnson Daniels Agitationsskrift "Vartdagliga brod, Eller; Battre an Socialismen."* Duluth: Skandinaviska Socialistklubben, Duluth (West End) Local, [191–?]. 15 p. In Swedish.
    Photocopy. Original in Arbet-arrolesens Arkiv, Stockholm.

17. Public Ownership (Socialist) Party. [Handbill]. Duluth, 1912. (Duluth)
    Announcing Socialist meeting and parade in Duluth.

18. *St. Paul Trades and Labor Assembly. Legislative Committee. The Peoples Voice.* St. Paul, [ca. 1910s]. (Mnradpam)
    Campaign circular for labor-endorsed candidates.

1914

19. Mills, Ethelwyn. *Legislative Program of the Socialist Party: Record of the Work of the Socialist Representatives in the State Legislatures of the United States, 1899–1913.* Chicago: Socialist Party, National Office, 1914. 64 p.

1916

20. Maley, Anna Agnes. *Our National Kitchen: The Substance of a Speech on Socialism.* Minneapolis: The People's Press, 1916. 62 p.

21. Shutter, Marion D. *Socialism: Its Purpose and Program.* Minneapolis: Printing Club Press, Church of the Redeemer, 1916. 27 p.

22. Suomalaisen Sosialistijarton Keskipiiri. *Viidennen Edustajakokouksen Poytakirja, Tehty Superiorissa, Wis., Helmikuun 3, 4, 5, 9 ja 10 Paivina, 1916.* Superior: Työmies, 1916. 83 p. In Finnish.

23. Union Campaign Committee. *City Campaign News.* Minneapolis, 1916. On microfilm.
    Campaign circular in form of newspaper profiles Thomas Van Lear.

1917

24. Brown, Rome G. *The Socialist Menace to Constitutional Government.* Minneapolis: Review Pub. Co., 1917. 22 p.
    Annual address delivered before the Louisiana State Bar Assn. at Alexandria, La., May 12, 1917.

25. Gordon, Fred G. *Bolshevism, Seventy Years Old: Not Produced by Poverty, Unemployment or Autocracy, Originated by Karl Marx and Frederic Engels in 1847: Must Be Combated by Presentation of Facts, Logic and History.* Minneapolis: American Committee of Minneapolis, [1917]. 7 p.

26. Labor's Municipal Nonpartisan League. *Platform and Candidates Endorsed by Labor's Municipal Nonpartisan League.* Minneapolis, [1917]. 4 p. (Mnradpam)

27. *Socialism Is Real Menace in Our State Now.* N.p., [1917?]. 8 p.

1918

28. American Committee of Minneapolis. *The Real Marx Doctrines.* Minneapolis, [1918]. 2 p.

29. American Committee of Minneapolis. *Where Spargo Stands.* Minneapolis, [1918]. [4 p.]
    Attack on Socialist author John Spargo.

30. *Are You Ready to Hand Over Your Farm to a Bunch of Socialist Adventurers?: That Is What Townleyism Means, Mr. Farmer.* N.p., [1918?]. 11 p.

31. Citizens Alliance of Minneapolis. *Arbitration Order No. 30 Issued by the Minnesota Commission of Public Safety Following Governor Burnquist's Proclamation of Mar. 30, 1918, Relating to Employment of Labor during the War.* [Minneapolis, 1918]. 8 p.

32. Hanson, Ole. *What Ole Says.* Minneapolis: American Committee of Minneapolis, 1918. 4 p.

33. National Nonpartisan League. *Let the People Rule in Minnesota.* St. Paul: C. W. Barnes, [1918]. 8 p. (Mnradpam)
    Endorses Charles A. Lindbergh, Sr., for governor. Includes platform and lists other candidates.

34. National Nonpartisan League. Minnesota Branch. *Platform and Declaration of Principles.* St. Paul, 1918. 4 p. (Mnradpam)

35. Shutter, Marion D. *The Citizen and Political Socialism in Minneapolis.* Minneapolis: Women's Association, 1918. 20 p.

36. *Socialism Has Openly Challenged Americanism!* [St. Paul]: N.p., [1918 or 1920]. (Mnradpam)
    Campaign circular for St. Paul Mayor Larry Hodgson, labeling opponent William Mahoney and other "Labor candidates" socialists.

37. Socialist Party. [Poster]. Minneapolis, [1918]. (Mnradpam)
    Caroline Lowe, "a talented woman lawyer," to speak on "Labor in Politics."

38. Wood, Henry A. Wise. *The Workingman and the US Constitution.* Minneapolis: American Committee of Minneapolis, [1918]. 4 p.

1919

39. American Committee of Minneapolis. *Breaking Up the Family.* Minneapolis, 1919. 4 p.

40. American Committee of Minneapolis. *From the Report of the United States Senate Committee on Bolshevism.* Minneapolis, 1919. 10 p.

41. American Committee of Minneapolis. *Russia or America? Choose!* Minneapolis, 1919. 6 p.

42. American Committee of Minneapolis. *Tom Mooney's Case: Plainly and Briefly Told for the Busy Man who Wants the Truth: An Answer to the $1,000,000 Propaganda.* Minneapolis, [1919?]. [8 p.]

43. *Amerikan Unionismin Historiallinen Katekismus.* Duluth: Workers Socialist Pub. Co., [191–?]. 128 p. In Finnish.
    Finnish translation of *A Historical Catechism of American Unionism.*

44. Brier, Ernest. *Russian Workmen Have Neither Food nor Liberty: Spies Trail Them and Penalty of Death Threatens.* Minneapolis: American Committee of Minneapolis, [1919]. 8 p.

45. Brown, Rome G. *The Meaning of Socialism.* Minneapolis: American Committee of Minneapolis, [1919]. 14 p.

46. Cleary, Rev. J. M. *Socialism, the Enemy of Labor.* Minneapolis: American Committee of Minneapolis, [191–?]. [6 p.]

47. Collins, Peter W. *The Truth about Socialism.* Minneapolis: American Committee of Minneapolis, 1919. 15 p.

48. Collins, Peter W. *What Is Socialism?* Minneapolis: American Committee of Minneapolis, 1919; Fargo, N.Dak.: Independent Voters' Assn., 1919. 16 p.

49. Collins, Peter W. *Why Socialism Is Opposed to the Labor Movement.* Minneapolis: American Committee of Minneapolis, 1919. 16 p.

50. DeLeon, Daniel. *Socialist Reconstruction of Society: The Industrial Vote.* New York: Socialist Labor Party, 1919. 48 p.

> Address delivered July 10, 1905, in Union Temple, Minneapolis. First edition published in 1905 under title *Preamble of the Industrial Workers of the World.*

51. Fenton, Josiah. *The Blasphemous Catechism of the Alien Socialists.* Minneapolis: American Anti-Socialist League, 1919. 6 p.

52. Fenton, Josiah. *Down with the Scars and Stripes: How Socialism Insults the Flag: To Hell with Your Flag.* Minneapolis: American Anti-Socialist League, 1919. 4 p.

53. Gordon, Fred G. *The Case Against Socialism.* Minneapolis: American Anti-Socialist League, 1919. 5 p.

54. O'Reilly, Father ——. *Labor in Danger.* Minneapolis: American Committee of Minneapolis, [191–?]. [2 p.]

55. People's Franchise Bureau. *Where Will You Be Tuesday? With the Constructionists or Will You Be with the Destructionists?* Minneapolis: The Bureau, 1919. 1 sheet.

56. Sargent, Noel. *The Socialism of 1919.* Minneapolis: The Author, 1919. 21 p.

57. Schmahl, Julius August. [Address]. Minneapolis: Syndicate Print Co., 1919. 21 p.

> Address given at New Ulm, Aug. 20, 1919, and Kimball, Sept. 27, 1919, for the homecoming of World War I soldiers and the 57th anniversary of the "repulse of the Sioux Indians."

58. Shutter, Marion D. *From Constitution to Chaos in Russia.* Minneapolis: American Committee of Minneapolis, 1919. 21 p.

59. Shutter, Marion D. *The Menace of Socialism.* Minneapolis: American Committee of Minneapolis, [1919]. 20 p.

60. Shutter, Marion D. *Socialism and the Family.* Minneapolis: American Committee of Minneapolis, 1919. 16 p.

> Address before the State Federation of Women's Clubs, Little Falls, Sept. 24, 1919.

61. Shutter, Marion D. *Some Recent Developments in Socialism.* Minneapolis: Women's Association, [191–?]. 18 p.

> "Reprinted by the Women's Association."

62. Socialist Party. [Handbill]. Minneapolis, 1919. (Mnradpam)

> A. E. Latimer to speak on the National War Labor Board as part of the Socialist Lecture Course Series.

63. Working People's Nonpartisan Political League. *Minnesota Labor Is about to Vote for Itself.* Minneapolis, [1919?]. 7 p.

1920

64. Ebert, Justus. *Teollisuusunionismi Teoriana Ja Kaytannossa.* Duluth: Workers Socialist Pub. Co., [1920?]. 127 p. In Finnish.

> Translation of *The I.W.W. in Theory and Practice.*

65. For Home and Country League. *Mass Meeting.* St. Paul, 1920. (Mnradpam)

> Handbill announcing antisocialist rally.

66. For Home and Country League. *Will You Vote for Socialism, or Will You Vote for Americanism?* St. Paul, [1919 or 1920]. 1 sheet.

67. Gordon, F[red] R. G. *The Winnipeg Strike: Red Radicals Attempt Soviet Revolution: Statement of Facts by a Man Who Was There.* Minneapolis: American Committee of Minneapolis, [192–?]. 12 p.

68. Minneapolis Tribune. *Dinner by the Minneapolis Tribune to Minnesota Editorial Association . . . Toasts and Responses.* Minneapolis: The Tribune, 1920. 24 p.

> Antisocialist, anti-NPL speeches. Rome G. Brown was toastmaster at the West Hotel, Minneapolis, Feb. 27, 1920.

69. Nielson, Minnie J. *A Message to Minnesota Womanhood: Minnie J. Nielson, State Superintendent of Schools* *of North Dakota, Relates Her Experiences and Says . . . .* St. Paul: Minnesota Sound Government Assn., [1920]. 8 p.

70. Sargent, Noel. *Socialism, the Farmer, the Nonpartisan League.* St. Paul: Minnesota Sound Government Assn., [1920]. 8 p.

71. Shutter, Marion D. *The United States and the Warning from Russia.* Minneapolis: Women's Association, Printing Club Press, Church of the Redeemer, [1920]. 23 p.

1921

72. Brown, Robert L., and Chas. Streetly. *How about the City Council?* Minneapolis: The Authors, 1921. 1 sheet.

73. Lenin, Vladimir Ilich. *Pientuotannosta Yhteiskunnalliseen Tuotantoon.* Duluth: Workers Socialist Pub. Co., 1921. 31 p. In Finnish.

74. Minneapolis Trades and Labor Assembly. *A Statement of Facts to the General Public.* Minneapolis: Minneapolis Building Trades Council, 1921. 15 p.

75. St. Paul Trades and Labor Assembly. *The Truth about Organized Labor: An Official Refutation of the Charges Made against Organized Labor.* St. Paul, 1921. 16 p.

76. Voters Information Club. *Some Things the Local Czars of Socialism Fail to Mention.* Minneapolis: Political Committee of the Voters Information Club, 1921. 15 p.

77. Working Peoples Political League. City Central Committee. *Voters! Which Do You Want? Minneapolis Home Rule or Government by St. Paul Commission . . .* Minneapolis, [1921]. 1 p.
Urges voters to vote for Thomas Van Lear.

1922

78. Agricultural Workers Industrial Union. *Helppotajuista Talousoppia, Maanviljelystyolaisten Teollisussunion Kasvatustoimiston Julkaisema.* Duluth: Workers Social-

ist Pub. Co., 1922. 60 p. In Finnish.
Translation of a publication of the Educational Department, IWW Agricultural Workers Union.

79. Carney, Jack. *Mary Marcy.* Chicago: Chas. Kerr and Co., 1922. 15 p. (Duluth)
Tribute to Marcy (1877–1922), socialist and author.

80. Citizens Alliance, [Duluth]. *Special Bulletin.* Duluth, 1922. 2 p. (Duluth)
An Aug. 28, 1922, bulletin concerning Duluth's economic development and labor movement.

81. Preus, J. A. O. *A Government Experiment versus Life Insurance Principles.* N.p., [1922]. 21 p.
Address delivered by Governor Preus to the annual meeting of Life Insurance Presidents, New York, Dec. 9, 1921. The "government experiment" of the title refers to the "socialism" rampant in North Dakota and Minnesota politics.

1923

82. Citizens Alliance of Minneapolis. *Go to Hell.* Minneapolis, 1923. [12 p.] (Mnradpam)
Pamphlet prints excerpts from the *Minneapolis Labor Review* to create propaganda against the labor movement.

83. Minnesota. Legislature. Senate. Special Investigating Committee. *The Red Menace in Minnesota: An Open Letter to Friends of Constitutional Government in Minnesota.* St. Paul, [1923]. 36 p.
Includes transcripts of Harry Curran Wilbur's and W. O. Washburn's testimony before the senate investigating committee.

1924

84. Soltis, John Gabriel. *Political Traitors and How They Work: Astounding Revelation of Treason Within the Labor Movement.* Minneapolis: The Author, 1924. 29 p.

85. Votaw, O. R. *Save the Farmer-Labor Party! Elect J[ulius] F. Emme to Congress.* [St. Paul, 1924]. 4 p. (Mnradpam)
Statement by the Worker's Party of America, St. Paul

City Central Committee, about its support for the F-LP. Urges voters to vote for William Z. Foster for president, Benjamin Gitlow for vice-president, and other F-LP candidates.

86. Working People's Political League. *Labor-Progressive Candidates: Vote for These Men for Nomination.* St. Paul, 1924. 1 sheet. (Mnradpam)

Handbill lists St. Paul candidates, with photos. Reverse side announces rally.

1925

87. Citizen's Alliance of St. Paul. *"Five Years": Showing What Has Been Accomplished in Improving Industrial Relations in Saint Paul.* [St. Paul, 1925?]. [27 p.]

1926

88. Citizens Alliance of Ramsey and Dakota Counties. *Open Shop Construction in St. Paul: Some Representative Examples.* [St. Paul, 1926]. 48 p.

89. Citizens Alliance of St. Paul. *Proof.* St. Paul: Webb Pub. Co., [1926?]. 32 p.

Address delivered by Col. William Frew Long, general manager of the American Planners Assn. of Cleveland, at the sixth annual meeting of the Citizens Alliance.

1927

90. Dunne, William F. *The Threat to the Labor Movement: The Conspiracy Against the Trade Unions: Efficiency Unions for the Bosses or Effective Unions for the Workers.* [New York?]: N.p., [1927]. 40 p.

1928

91. Socialist Party. [Letter]. St. Paul, 1928. (Mnradpam)

Letter sent to friends of the party regarding Norman Thomas's presidential bid and the formation of a local branch of the party in St. Paul on May 2, 1928.

92. Socialist Party of Minnesota. *To the Thinking Voter.* Minneapolis, [1928]. 1 sheet.

1930

93. Communist Party. District 9. *Support the Candidates of Class Struggle—Vote Communist.* Minneapolis, [1930]. 1 sheet. (Mnradpam)

Prints copy of unemployment insurance bill. Lists Communist candidates, including Karl Reeve for governor and Rudolph Harju for U.S. Senator.

1931

94. Citizens Alliance of Ramsey and Dakota Counties. *Official List of the Firms in St. Paul in the Building Construction Lines who Conduct Their Business on the American Plan of Employment.* [St. Paul, 1931]. 26 p.

95. *Demonstrate for Immediate Unemployment Relief at the State Capitol.* N.p., [1931]. 1 sheet. (Mnradpam)

Handbill announcing demonstration, Jan. 7, 1931.

96. Workers and Farmers Cooperative Unity Alliance. *Osuustoiminta, Trotskilaisuus ja Tyotatekevien Yhtenaisyys* (Cooperativism, Trotskyism and Their Connection to the Worker). Superior: Työmies Print, [1930s]. 30 p. In Finnish. (IHRC)

1932

97. American Federation of Labor. Rank and File Committee for Communist Candidates. [Handbill]. N.p., [1932?]. 1 sheet. (Mnradpam)

Announcing a Communist political rally. Gubernatorial candidate William Schneiderman and congressional candidate Morris Karson to speak.

98. Citizens Alliance of Minneapolis. *The Citizens Alliance Free Employment Bureau of Minneapolis, Minnesota.* [Minneapolis, 1932]. 12 p.

99. City Campaign Committee for Worker Ticket. *Support the Workers' Ticket.* N.p., [1932?]. 4 p. (Mnradpam)

Prints the Workers' party municipal election platform for Minneapolis. Endorsed by the Communist party.

100. Communist Party of the United States of America. District 9 Election Campaign Committee. *Workers' and Farmers' Voice.* Minneapolis, [1932]. On microfilm.

Campaign circular in form of newspaper. Contained profiles of Communist candidates and platform.

101. Eggert, A. L. *The People's Voice.* St. Paul, 1932. (Mnradpam)

Campaign circular for labor-endorsed candidates.

102. [Mahoney Volunteer Committee]. [Campaign leaflets]. St. Paul, 1932–42. (Mnradpam)

Campaign leaflets on behalf of William Mahoney for mayoral and congressional races. Issued by different individuals and groups.

1933

103. Nygard, Emil. *America's First Red Mayor in Action.* New York: Workers Library Publishers, 1933. 15 p.

"Address of Emil Nygard, Communist mayor of Crosby, Minn., Webster Hall, New York City, Thursday, October 19th, 1933."

1934

104. Citizens Alliance of Minneapolis. *The Citizens Alliance of Minneapolis: What It Is, What It Stands For, What It Does, What People Think of It.* [Minneapolis, mid-1930s?]. (Mnradpam)

105. Communist Party of the United States of America. *Prepare for Strike! Support the Drivers.* Minneapolis, 1934. 1 sheet. (Mnradpam)

Handbill announcing a mass rally in support of the July truck drivers' strike.

106. Democratic State Central Committee. *Take No Chances.* Duluth, [1934]. 1 p. (Mnradpam)

Anti-Communist campaign circular for Democratic gubernatorial candidate, John Regan. Uses religion to red-bait opponent Floyd Olson.

107. Dunne, William F., and Morris Childs. *Permanent Counter-Revolution: The Role of the Trotskyites in the Minneapolis Strikes.* New York: Workers Library Publishers, 1934. 55 p.

108. Emery, Robert C. *Thirty Years From Now.* St. Paul: The Author, 1934. 63 p.

This is a fictive account of life in Minnesota under a Communist regime, which had risen to power after the 1934 election. Distributed by the State Anti-Communist Society, 1845 St. Clair St., St. Paul.

109. General Drivers and Helpers Union, Local 574 [Teamsters]. *Working Men and Women of Minneapolis . . .* Minneapolis, 1934. 2 p. (Mnradpam)

Handbill explains the strike, highlights the role of the Citizens Alliance in it, and announces a mass rally at the Minneapolis parade ground in support of the truck drivers.

110. Griffith, L. L. *The Capitalist Rooster.* St. Paul: Farmer-Labor Assn., [1934?]. 11 p. (Mnradpam)

Reprinted from the *Farmer-Labor Leader.* Fable of capitalism's pitfalls.

111. International Labor Defense. *Hear the Leaders of the San Francisco General Strike.* [St. Paul?, 1934]. (Mnradpam)

Handbill announces an International Labor Defense rally on Oct. 7, 1934. Speakers include longshoreman Lloyd Stroud, Workers International Relief member Ed Royce (both members of the strike committee), and George Morris, editor of the *Western Worker,* the official strike newspaper.

112. Minnesota Socialist Party. *The Minnesota Socialist.* Minneapolis, 1934. On microfilm.

Newspaper served as campaign tool for Morris Kaplan, Socialist candidate for U.S. Senate. Also carried national news as it related to the party.

113. Olson for Governor All Party Volunteer Committee. *Bread or Straw: The Issues of the Campaign.* Minneapolis, 1934. 16 p.

114. Olson for Governor All Party Volunteer Committee. *Gov. Olson's Position on Free Text Books and Communism.* Minneapolis, [1934]. 1 p. (Mnradpam)

Response to red-baiting opponents.

115. Olson for Governor All Party Volunteer Committee. *The Truth about Free Text Books.* Minneapolis, [1934]. 14 p. (Mnradpam)

A poster advertising a Lenin Memorial Meeting in Minneapolis, 1939, featured African Americans William Patterson and Nellie Stone (later Nellie Stone Johnson). Half the ticket proceeds were to be donated to strike funds, and those planning to attend were asked to bring canned goods for strikers. The ephemeral nature of this kind of material is clear here: the poster has not survived, only the damaged negative and photograph taken of it.

116. Packing House Workers' Industrial Union. *Which Union?* South St. Paul, [1934]. (Mnradpam)

Handbill challenging the Amalgamated Meat Cutters' Union (AFL affiliated) to prove its accusations against the Packing House Workers' Industrial Union (Trade Union Unity League [TUUL] affiliated).

117. Socialist Party of Minnesota. *Socialism and Agriculture.* Minneapolis, [1934]. 4 p. (Mnradpam)

Campaign leaflet for U.S. Senate candidate Morris Kaplan.

118. Socialist Public Meeting. N.p.: [Socialist Party, 1934?]. (Mnradpam)

Handbill announcing speeches by Morris Kaplan, Socialist candidate for U.S. Senate, and Oscar Hawkins.

119. Young Communist League. District 9. *Whom Shall the Youth Support in the Election?* Minneapolis, [1934]. (Mnradpam)

Lists Communist candidates for state offices.

1935

120. Cannon, James P. *Who Killed Pat Corcoran and Why?* Minneapolis: Socialist Party of Minneapolis, [1935]. 1 sheet.

121. Citizens Alliance of Minneapolis. *Minneapolis Bureau of Industrial Relations: Its Purposes and Functions.* [Minneapolis, 1935]. 16 p.

122. Communist Party. *Vote for a Workers' Program and Militant Candidates!* Minneapolis, [1935?]. 4 p. (Mnradpam)

Pamphlet discusses the failure of a united labor front with the F-LP. Includes profile of Alfred Tiala, Communist candidate for mayor in Minneapolis, and the Communist party program.

123. Dunne, William F. *The Supreme Court's Challenge to Labor: The N.I.R.A. Decision: A Signal for Intensified Attacks on the Workers.* New York: Workers Library Publishers, 1935. 22 p.

Issued by the Communist Party of the United States of America.

124. Election Campaign Committee for Chas. Strong and Myrtle Strong. *Program of the Communist Party in the Duluth Municipal Election.* Duluth, [1935?]. 4 p. (Duluth)

1936

125. Brunson, H. S. *Think! Read! Show This to Your Neighbors.* St. Paul, [1936?]. (Mnradpam)

Anti-Communist poster linking Ernest Lundeen, F-L candidate for the U.S. Senate, to Communists. Brunson was secretary of the American Anti-Communist Assn.

126. Citizens Alliance of Ramsey and Dakota Counties. *The Citizens Alliance of Ramsey and Dakota Counties: Its Platform and Its Function.* [St. Paul, 1936]. 18 p.

127. Communist Party of the United States of America. *Communist Election Platform.* New York: Workers Library Pub. Co., 1936. 16 p. (Mnradpam)

Includes Communist party platform and profiles of presidential candidate Earl R. Browder and running mate James Ford. Back of pamphlet urges voters to vote for F-L candidates in Minnesota.

128. Communist Party of the United States of America. *The Next Step: Improve Your Conditions through Farmer-Labor Victory.* Minneapolis: CPUSA, [1936?]. 6 p.

129. Hathaway, Clarence A. *Problems in Our Farmer-Labor Activities.* N.p., [1936]. 7 p. (Mnradpam)

Article reprinted from *The Communist,* May 1936, p. 427–33.

130. Minnesota Committee in Support of American Democracy. *Are We Awake to What Is Happening in Minnesota? Is Communism Establishing a Popular Front in This State?* St. Paul, 1936. 4 p. (Mnradpam)

131. Olson for Governor All Party Volunteer Committee. *Keep Government for the People!* Minneapolis, [1936]. [15 p.] (Mnradpam)

Campaign pamphlet discusses Governor Floyd B. Olson's program for the state.

132. Socialist Party. *Hear Norman Thomas on the Farmer-Labor Democratic Alliance.* St. Paul, 1936. (Mnradpam)

Circular announcing speech by Norman Thomas, Socialist presidential candidate, in St. Paul. (President Roosevelt visited St. Paul on the same day and spoke to 50,000 people at the State Capitol. Later that night Thomas gave the Socialist response.)

133. Socialist Party. (U.S.). *1936 Platform.* Minneapolis, 1936. 6 p.

134. Shutter, Marion. *Under Which Flag? Flag Day Address, Sunday, June 14, 1936.* Minneapolis: Women's Association, [1936]. 15 p.

Anti-Communist speech.

135. State Republican Volunteer Committee. [Leaflets]. St. Paul, [1936]. (Mnradpam)

Series of 24 anti-Communist leaflets attacking the F-LP. Titles include: "Sound Liberalism," "Ernest Lundeen: Who Likes Russia Much Better than America," and "Buddies and Bedfellows: Communist F-L Tie-Up."

136. *Tyovaen Taskukalenteri, 1937.* Duluth: Workers' Socialist Pub. Co., 1936. 127 p. In Finnish.

137. Workers Alliance of Hennepin County. *Meet the Challenge!* Minneapolis, [1936]. (Mnradpam)

Handbill announcing mass meeting about WPA cuts. Sander Genis to speak.

1937

138. Benson, Elmer. *Mobilizing for Peace.* [Minneapolis?]: Minnesota Student Alliance, Minnesota Youth Assembly, Minnesota All University Peace Council, 1937. 8 p. (Mnradpam)

Governor Elmer Benson's address at the University of Minnesota's Student Peace Demonstration, Apr. 22, 1937.

139. Communist Party of St. Paul. [Handbill]. [St. Paul, 1937?]. (Mnradpam)

Announcing a rally at the Italian Consulate at 5th and Cedar in St. Paul to protest the German/Italian invasion of Spain.

140. Communist Party of the United States of America. Hennepin County Committee. [Letter]. Minneapolis, 1937. (Mnradpam)

Letter from Erik Bert to friends of the party, clarifying the party's position on the F-LP and announcing meetings and rallies. Attached is a ticket to a mass meeting challenging the Citizens Alliance.

141. McGaughern, W. J. *What Is the Issue?* N.p., [1937]. 7 p. (Mnradpam)

A transcript of a radio address on Communist infiltration in the election. Originally broadcast June 11, 1937.

142. Minneapolis Local of the Socialist Party. *The [Patrick J.] Corcoran Assassination and the Game of the Communist Party: Minneapolis—Watch the Fingers of the Frame-up Artists!* [Minneapolis, 1937]. 1 sheet.

143. Minnesota Communist Party. *Draft Resolution of the State Committee: Building the Communist Party in* *the Struggle for Trade Union Unity and an All-inclusive Farmer Labor Party.* Minneapolis, 1937. 10 p.

144. Minnesota Liberal Council. Executive Committee. *Minnesota Liberal Counselor: F-L Party Betrayed by Mexican Generals.* Minneapolis: The Committee, 1937. 4 p.

145. Minnesota People's Lobby. *The People's Lobbyist.* St. Paul, 1937. On microfilm.
  Issued only once (on Apr. 1, 1937) to report the upcoming statewide rally at the Capitol on Apr. 4 and 5, 1937.

146. Minnesota Worker's Alliance. *Membership Book.* St. Paul, [1937?]. 12 p. (Mnradpam)

147. North American Committee to Aid Spanish Democracy. Minneapolis Unit. *Spain Speaks.* Minneapolis, [late 1930s]. (Mnradpam)
  Handbill announcing a mass rally to aid the Spanish Republic.

148. Ramsey County Farmer-Labor Association. *The People's Voice.* St. Paul, 1937. (Mnradpam)
  Campaign circular for labor-endorsed candidates.

149. *A Statement of Recent Developments in the Minneapolis Labor Movement.* [Minneapolis, 1937]. 2 p.
  Speakers at this mass meeting included Leslie Sinton, John Boscoe, and Ray Dunne. Discussion about Teamsters Local 544.

150. *The Sunday Worker: A Minneapolis Election Edition.* New York: Comprodaily Pub. Co., 1937. 16 p. (Mnradpam)

151. Workers Alliance of Ramsey County. *Unemployed and WPA Working Men and Women—DEMONSTRATE.* St. Paul, 1937. (Mnradpam)
  Handbill announcing rally.

1938

152. Benson for Governor All Party Volunteer Committee. *Forgery! Frame-up! Republican Plot Exposed!* Minneapolis, [1937 or 1938]. 4 p.
  Circular responds to photos published in *Are They Communists or Catspaws?* that showed Governor Benson with alleged Communists and Communist sympathizers. Claims photos were faked.

153. Chase, Ray Park. *Are They Communists or Catspaws? A Red-Baiting Article.* Anoka: The Author, 1938. 60 p.
  Controversial article, which Chase published as a booklet, evoked many responses and commentaries.

154. Communist Party of the United States of America. *Communist Election Platform, 1938: For Jobs, Security, Democracy, and Peace.* New York: Workers Library Publishers, 1938. 15 p.
  Issued for Minnesota State Committee, Communist party.

155. Dunne, V. R. *The Farmer Labor Party: A Program: An Open Letter to Governor Benson.* [Minneapolis?]: Minnesota Section, Socialist Workers Party, 1938. 15 p. (Mnradpam)

156. Farmer-Labor Women's Federation of Minnesota. *A Call to the Women of Minnesota.* [St. Paul?, 1938]. 4 p. (Mnradpam)

157. Inter-Church Mother's Volunteer Committee. *So That the People May Know.* Minneapolis, [1938]. 2 p. (Mnradpam)
  Anti-Communist literature attacks state representative candidate Lucy Lawson.

158. Socialist Labor Party. *Vote Socialist Labor Party.* St. Paul, [1938]. 4 p. (Mnradpam)
  The state platform announcing that the party will run John W. Castle for governor under the Industrial party banner.

159. Socialist Workers Party. *Down with the War Machine.* New York, 1938. 4 p. (Mnradpam)

160. Socialist Workers Party. Minneapolis Branch. *Join the Socialist Workers Party: Vote the Union Ticket.* [Minneapolis: The Party, 1938?]. 6 p.
  How the party views the city elections in 1938.

161. United Liberal Voters Council. *Here Is the Proof.* Minneapolis, [1938?]. 4 p. (Mnradpam)
  Booklet is part of a red-baiting campaign against Governor Benson, which began when Ray Chase published photos of the governor with alleged Communists and Communist sympathizers in *Are They Communists or Catspaws?* The governor responded in a circular entitled *Forgery! Frame-up!,* which

asserted that the photos were faked. *Here Is the Proof* answers these accusations and attempts to show that the photos are in fact real.

1939

162. *Do You Want Your Boy To Go to War?* N.p., [1939?]. (Mnradpam)

Handbill announcing rally against the war. Louis Budenz, editor of the *Chicago Record,* to speak.

163. [Harris/Fine Volunteer Committee]. *A Progressive Victory Means More Jobs and Better Living.* Minneapolis, 1939. (Mnradpam)

Campaign leaflet for Communist candidates: Lem Harris for school board, Fred Fine for park board.

164. Joint Committee of the Building and Construction Trades Council of Minneapolis. *Protest Mass Meeting.* Minneapolis, [1939?]. (Mnradpam)

Handbill announcing rally protesting WPA cuts.

165. Ostby, Roger B. *Will Minnesota Submit to a Rule by Force and Violence?* Albert Lea: The Author, 1939. 16 p.

Photocopy. Original at Tamiment Institute Library, New York.

166. Rondo Local Workers Alliance. *Attention Unemployed and WPA Workers.* St. Paul, 1939. (Mnradpam)

Handbill announcing a mass meeting at Welcome Hall in St. Paul.

167. Tom Mooney Molders Defense Committee. *Welcome Tom Mooney.* [St. Paul?], 1939. (Mnradpam)

Handbill announcing meeting at which Tom Mooney will speak.

168. United Packinghouse Workers. [CIO newletters]. South St. Paul, 1939. (Mnradpam)

Series of six CIO newletters issued by different locals at different meat-packing plants, including Armour, Swift, and Cudahy.

169. United Voters League. *Do You Want 544 To Run Minneapolis?* [Minneapolis?, 1939]. (Mnradpam)

Anti-Communist campaign poster connecting Minneapolis candidates T. A. Eide and Glen Wallace to Teamsters Local 544.

170. Workers Alliance. *Fight Against Relief Cuts.* [St. Paul?, 1939?]. (Mnradpam)

Handbill announcing mass meeting about WPA cuts. William Mahoney to speak.

171. Workers Alliance of Ramsey County. *Fight Fallon's Relief Cuts.* St. Paul, 1939. (Mnradpam)

Handbill announcing mass meeting at the German American Auditorium in St. Paul. Chester Watson, William Mahoney, and others to speak.

172. Workers Alliance of Ramsey County. *Free Movies.* St. Paul, 1939. (Mnradpam)

Handbill announcing two free movies sponsored by the WPA in St. Paul.

173. Workers Alliance of Ramsey County. Protest Action Committee. *Daily Bulletin of the Protest Action Committee.* St. Paul, 1939. (Mnradpam)

Daily bulletin of the WPA strike. (Note: MHS has several issues.)

174. Workers Alliance of Ramsey County. Protest Action Committee. *A Letter to the Packing House Workers.* St. Paul, 1939. (Mnradpam)

Circular discussing the WPA strike and requesting support from the packinghouse workers in South St. Paul.

175. Workers Benefit Association. *Strike Bulletin!* [Minneapolis, 1939]. (Mnradpam)

Concerning the WPA strike. Organization seems to be the Minneapolis equivalent of the Protest Action Committee in St. Paul.

176. Young Communist League. *Peace, Jobs and Civil Liberties!* Minneapolis, [1939–40?]. 4 p. (Mnradpam)

Antiwar pamphlet announcing youth rally and Liebknecht Memorial Meeting at Pioneer Hall on Rondo St., St. Paul.

177. Young Communist League. Kenny Brown Club. *Make Friday the 13th Your Lucky Day and the War-Mongers Unlucky Day!* St. Paul, [1939]. (Mnradpam)

Handbill announces antiwar symposium. Kenny Brown of St. Paul was a member of the league who died in the Spanish Civil War.

1940

178. *Behind the 544 Suit: The Truth about the Fink Suit against the Minneapolis General Drivers Union.* Minneapolis: Minneapolis Teamsters Joint Council, 1940. 38 p.

Foreword by Miles Dunne. The pamphlet reprints a series of articles originally published in the *Northwest Organizer,* the teamsters' official newspaper.

179. Benson for Senator Volunteer Committee. *The Minnesota Crisis!* St. Paul, 1940. On microfilm.

Campaign circular in newspaper form. Smear campaign against U.S. Senate candidate Henrik Shipstead.

180. Communist Party. *Tune In Every Friday 10:15 PM Sept. 6 to Nov. 8, 1940, 1370 on Your Dial, WMIN : For Peace, Jobs, Security, Civil Rights.* Minneapolis, [1940]. 1 p.

181. Communist Party. Rondo Branch. *Should the U.S. Enter the War?* [St. Paul?, 1940?]. (Mnradpam)

Mimeographed leaflet announcing meeting and discussion about the war.

182. Communist Party of the United States of America. Election Committee. *The Campaigner.* Minneapolis, [1940–41?]. On microfilm.

Newspaper printed for campaign purposes. Profiled Communist party candidates and regularly printed party platform. (Note: MHS has Aug.–Sept. 1940 and Oct. 1941.)

183. Communist Party of the United States of America. Minnesota State Committee. *Who Defends the Interests of the Finnish People?* Minneapolis, [1939 or 1940]. 1 p. (Mnradpam)

184. Communist Party of the United States of America. National Election Campaign Committee. *To Make Your Vote Count, Vote Communist.* N.p., [1940?]. (Mnradpam)

Card listing Communist candidates in Minnesota.

185. Progressive Bookshop. *Censored by the War Press.* Minneapolis, [1940?]. (Mnradpam)

Statement about civil liberties and freedom of the press. Reprinted from the *Daily Worker,* Jan. 5, 1940.

186. *Rose Tillotson for Mayor—Robert Turner for Council Volunteer Committee. Peace . . . Civil Liberties . . . Jobs.* St. Paul, [1940?]. 4 p. (Mnradpam)

Campaign circular for Communist party candidates in St. Paul mayoral and city council races.

187. Socialist Labor Party. *1940 Platform.* St. Paul, 1940. 7 p. (Mnradpam)

188. Socialist Workers Party. *Support the Anti-War Candidate for United States Senator—Dr. Grace Carlson.* St. Paul, 1940. (Mnradpam)

Handbill for the candidate.

189. Socialist Workers Party. Twin Cities Branches. *Twin City Memorial Meeting.* Minneapolis, 1940. (Mnradpam)

Handbill announcing memorial meeting for Leon Trotsky.

190. Watson for Congress Campaign Committee. *Equality to Live—Not—Equality to Die!* [St. Paul?, 1940?]. (Mnradpam)

Handbill announcing Chester Watson to speak on race discrimination.

1941

191. Communist Party of the United States of America. Minnesota State Committee. *German Fascism Opens Criminal War against Socialist Soviet Republic.* Minneapolis, 1941. (Mnradpam)

Statement by William Z. Foster and Robert Minor. Reprinted from the *Daily Worker,* Aug. 2, 1941.

192. Novack, George E. *The Bill of Rights in Danger! The Meaning of the Minneapolis Convictions.* Foreword by James Farrell. New York: Civil Rights Defense Committee, [1941]. 14 p.

193. Novack, George E. *Witchhunt in Minnesota: The Federal Prosecution of the Socialist Workers Party and Local 544, CIO.* New York: Civil Rights Defense Committee, [1941?]. 23 p.

194. Socialist Workers Party. Twin Cities Branches. *Twin City Sunday Forum Announces James P. Cannon.* Minneapolis, 1941. (Mnradpam)

Handbill announces speech by Cannon entitled,

"Why We Are on Trial," about the sedition trials in Minneapolis. Also announces future speakers at the weekly forum.

195. Volunteer Committee for Helen Allison Winter. *Books Not Bullets.* Minneapolis, 1941. 4 p. (Mnradpam)

Campaign leaflet for Winter, Communist candidate for Minneapolis Library Board. Endorsed by the Young Communist League.

196. Volunteer Committee for Helen Allison Winter. *For Peace and Progress.* Minneapolis, [1941?]. 5 p. (Mnradpam)

Campaign leaflet for Winter, Communist candidate for Minneapolis Library Board.

1942

197. Cannon, James P. *Socialism on Trial: The Official Court Record of James P. Cannon's Testimony in the Famous Minneapolis "Sedition" Trial.* New York: Pioneer Publishers, 1942. 116 p.

198. Chase, Ray Park. *Shall Private Enterprise Be Destroyed and the Right to Work for Profit Be Taken from Free Men and Women?* Anoka: The Author, 1942. 70 p.

Accuses the Farm Security Administration and Farm Credit Administration of being Communist fronts.

199. Communist Party of the United States of America. Minnesota Election Campaign Committee. *Program for Victory.* Minneapolis, 1942. 4 p. (Mnradpam)

Campaign literature for Communist candidates.

200. Communist Party of the United States of America. Minnesota State Committee. *Vote for Victory.* Minneapolis, [1942]. (Mnradpam)

Campaign pamphlet urging voters to support the "win-the-war" candidates.

201. [Communist Party of the United States of America. Minnesota State Committee]. *What More Can You Do to Win the War.* [Minneapolis?, 1941–45?]. 1 p. (Mnradpam)

202. Goldman, Albert. *In Defense of Socialism: The Official Court Record of Albert Goldman's Final Speech for the Defense in the Famous Minneapolis "Sedition" Trial.* New York: Pioneer Publishers, 1942. 95 p.

203. Twin Cities Ordnance Plant, Local 1152. *TCOP-UE-CIO Leader.* Minneapolis, 1942. 1 sheet.

One side reprinted a page of *UE News* (national edition), the other side urged women at Twin Cities Ordnance Plant to join the UE-CIO.

1943

204. Dunne, V. R. [Filing statement]. Minneapolis, 1943. [2 p.] (Mnradpam)

Dunne's statement of intent to run for Minneapolis mayor. Attached is a letter from Harry DeBoer, Dunne's campaign manager, that was mailed out to supporters, May 11, 1943.

205. United Electrical, Radio and Machine Workers of America, Local 1139. *Flash! United States Government through N.L.R.B. Examiner's Report finds Onan & Sons Co. Guilty.* Minneapolis, 1943. (Mnradpam)

Poster announces UE-CIO organizing drive at Onan & Sons Co. in Minneapolis, Apr. 6, 1943. Bill Mauseth to speak at meeting.

1944

206. America First Party. *Gerald L. K. Smith to Speak in St. Paul and Minneapolis.* N.p., [1944?]. (Mnradpam)

Handbill announcing speech and outlining America First principles.

207. Civil Rights Defense Committee. *Who Are the 18 Prisoners in the Minneapolis Labor Case?: How the "Gag" Act Has Endangered Workers Rights and Free Speech.* Foreword by James T. Farrell. New York: The Committee, 1944. 27 p.

208. Socialist Labor Party. [Handbill]. St. Paul, 1944. (Mnradpam)

Handbill announcing speech by Socialist Labor presidential candidate Edward Teichert, entitled "After the War! What?"

209. Socialist Workers Party. *Why We Are in Prison: Farewell Speeches of the 18 SWP and 544-CIO Minneapolis Prisoners.* New York: Pioneer Publishers, 1944. 54 p.

1947

210. Foote, Arthur. *Communists and Unitarians: A Sermon.* St. Paul: Unity Church, 1947. 7 p.

"Preached in Unity Church, St. Paul, January 19, 1947."

1948

211. Americans for Democratic Action. Minnesota Chapter. *What the Wallace Movement Means to the Progressives of Minnesota.* N.p., [1948]. 4 p. (Mnradpam)
Anti-Communist campaign circular. Unauthorized reprint of Communist party newsletter, *Action.* Attacks Henry Wallace.

212. Civil Rights Congress. *Your Rights Are at Stake!* [Minneapolis?, late 1940s]. (Mnradpam)
Handbill announcing a meeting about civil-rights violations by the Un-American Activities Committee. Hilda Eisler to speak.

213. Hennepin County DFL Volunteer Committee. *Will the DFL Party of Minnesota Be a Clean, Honest, Decent Progressive Party—or—Will It Be a COMMUNIST FRONT ORGANIZATION?* Minneapolis, [1948]. 15 p. (Mnradpam)

214. Independent Voters of Minnesota. *Program of the Independent Voters of Minnesota.* Minneapolis, [1948?]. 7 p. (Mnradpam)
Organization calls for united front of progressives and liberals to combat monopoly capitalism, imperialism, and armament and to work for civil and human rights.

215. [Socialist Workers Party]. *The Voice of Socialism: Radio Speeches by the Socialist Workers Party Candidates in the 1948 Election.* New York: Pioneer Publishers, [1948]. 31 p.
Speeches by Farrell Dobbs, Grace Carlson, and James Cannon.

216. Socialist Workers Party. *Vote for V. R. Dunne for U.S. Senator.* Minneapolis, 1948. 8 p. (Mnradpam)

1950

217. Citizens Good Government Committee. *Is Wier in Step with Anybody?* Minneapolis, [1950]. 1 p. (Mnradpam)
Links congressional candidate Roy Wier to Communist sympathizers Bill Mauseth and New York Congressman Vito Marcantonio.

218. *Halsted for Governor Committee. See the Proof that Communists Endorsed Harry H. Peterson.* Brainerd, 1950. 4 p. (Mnradpam)
Campaign circular for Charles L. Halsted, gubernatorial candidate, 1950. Accuses opponent of Communist connections.

219. Lindley for 3rd District Congress Volunteer Labor Committee. *Minneapolis Labor Stands Firmly Against Communism!* Minneapolis, [1950]. 1 p. (Mnradpam)
Campaign circular for Al Lindley, a Republican, accuses opponent Roy Wier of Communist connections.

220. *"We're for You, Wier . . ." says Minneapolis Labor, ". . . Because You Are Against Communism!"* [Minneapolis, 1950]. (Mnradpam)
Campaign poster issued in response to opponent Al Lindley's red-baiting literature in the congressional race.

1952

221. Central Labor Union of Minneapolis. [Program]. Minneapolis, 1952. 56 p.
Program for Labor Education Day, Apr. 29, 1952, Minneapolis Labor Temple.

1954

222. Socialist Labor Party. *Loyalty to What?* Minneapolis, 1954. 4 p. (Mnradpam)
Discussion of civil rights.

1957

223. Kirchman, Harry H. *Jungle Tom-Toms of Minnesota: or, State Communists' Latest Plot to Take Over Minnesota.* N.p.: The Author, 1957. 22 p.

224. Socialist Labor Party. *Common Sense and the H-Bomb.* Minneapolis, [1957?]. 4 p. (Mnradpam)

1960

225. Socialist Labor Party. *Survival Is the Issue!* Minneapolis, 1960. 4 p. (Mnradpam)
Platform of the party.

Newspapers

Entries describing radical-related newspapers are divided into three sections. The first lists newspapers that were openly affiliated with the Socialist or Communist parties. The second examines the labor press as it intersected with the traditionally defined radicalism of organized Socialist and Communist parties. The third concerns newspapers supporting the Farmer-Labor party and its predecessors, the Nonpartisan League and the Working People's Nonpartisan League, as they overlap with radical political parties. The location of each newspaper is indicated in the entry; most are in the collection of the Minnesota Historical Society (MHS) and are accessible on computerized catalog. A few of the titles are held at the Immigration History Research Center (IHRC).

For a more extensive description of the MHS-held titles, see "The Radical Press in Minnesota, 1900–1960: A Preliminary Survey of Minnesota Historical Society Holdings," by Elizabeth Raasch-Gilman and Matthew Mulcahy, available at the reference desk of the Research Center.

SOCIALIST AND COMMUNIST NEWSPAPERS

226. *Allarm*. Minneapolis: Scandinavian Propaganda League of the IWW, 1915–18. Monthly and semimonthly. In Swedish, Danish, and Norwegian.

Editors included Carl Ahlteen, Walfrid Engdahl, and Carl Skoglund. Succeeded *Solidaritet*, a short-lived Swedish IWW publication from Seattle. Paper covered events involving the IWW and the Scandinavian Socialist Federation in Minnesota and reported regularly on the unionization of workers in various industries. The paper opposed U.S. entry into World War I, and in 1917, Ahlteen and two others were arrested and charged with impeding the conduct of the war. The paper lost its second-class mailing permit and ceased in 1918. It was succeeded by *Facklan*.
MHS holdings: 1:12 (Dec. 1915)–4:9 (May 1, 1918)

227. *American Bolshevik*. Minneapolis: A. L. Sugarman, 1919–(?). Weekly.

Edited by A. L. Sugarman. Paper primarily covered city politics but reported occasionally on international and national labor news. Allied with the left wing of the Socialist party.
MHS holdings: 1:1–8 (Jan. [1]–Feb. 14, 1919)

228. *Eye-Opener*. Crookston: Public Ownership (Socialist) Party of the 9th Congressional District, 1911(?)–(?). Frequency unknown.

Edited and managed by A. Humble. Featured party news and platforms. Supported national Debs-Seidel ticket.
MHS holdings: 2:10 (July 5, 1912)

229. *Facklan* (The Torch). Minneapolis: Scandinavian Propaganda League of the IWW, 1918. Monthly. In Swedish.

This title succeeded *Allarm*, but it is believed that only one issue was published. Carl Ahlteen is listed as editor.
MHS holdings: 1:1 (Sept. 1918)

230. *Folkets Røst* (Voice of the People). Minneapolis: Emil Lauritz Mengshoel, 1918–25. Weekly. In Norwegian.

Published and edited by Emil Lauritz Mengshoel. Succeeded *Gaa Paa*. *Folkets Røst* was more moderate editorially than its predecessor. The paper denounced the civil-rights violations of the Red Scare but opposed the radicalization of the Minnesota Socialist party and viewed the burgeoning Communist party with some suspicion. Mengshoel continued to see himself as a Socialist even as he turned his attentions toward the F-LP. The paper gave complete and favorable coverage to the F-L movement.

MHS holdings: 1:1 (Dec. 21, 1918)–22:21 (Oct. 31, 1925)

231. *Gaa Paa* (Forward). Minneapolis: Emil Lauritz Mengshoel, 1903–18. Weekly. In Norwegian.

Emil Lauritz Mengshoel started the paper in Girard, Kans., in 1903 and moved it to Minneapolis in 1904. The paper was closely allied with the Socialist party and was, until 1911, the only Dano-Norwegian Socialist organ published at the time. The paper lost its second-class mailing permit in 1918, shortly before the end of World War I and ceased publication. Mengshoel resurrected the paper in December 1918 under the name of *Folkets Røst*.

MHS holdings: (?) 1903–15:39 (Oct. 26, 1918)

232. *Industrialisti.* Duluth: Workers Socialist Pub. Co., 1917–75. Daily. In Finnish.

Succeeded *Teollisuustyöläinen* (The Industrial Worker). Editors included Leo Laukki, Fred Jaakkola, Taavi Heino, William Risto, and Tobias Kekkonen. Managed by A. A. Toivonen. The paper generally followed the same policies as its predecessor but became officially the Finnish-language organ of the IWW and remained so through the 1960s. The paper was raided several times by the government, and in 1920 three of its editors were arrested and charged with criminal syndicalism.

MHS holdings: 1:2 (Mar. 19, 1917)–9:40 (Oct. 21, 1975)

233. *Labor Leader.* Duluth: Duluth Cooperative Society, 1917. Weekly.

Edited by William E. Reynolds. The paper was the official organ of the Socialist party in Duluth and Superior, founded by the antiwar wing of the party. It carried national news and a regular "Kiddy Korner" amidst its attacks on war profiteers, conscription, and imperialism. Also featured were stories on Japanese feminism, birth control, and sex education. The paper supported woman suffrage. Its pages provide a good picture of the social aspect of the Socialist party in the Twin Ports. In October 1917, it lost its second-class mailing permit. Succeeded by *Truth* in 1917.

MHS holdings: May 1–Oct. 5, 1917

234. *Minnesota Appeal.* Minneapolis: Socialist Workers Party, Minnesota Section, 1939(?)–(?). Frequency unknown.

Paper vehemently opposed President Franklin Roosevelt, the New Deal, and the Communist party, considering the Communist party to be a tool of the war-mongering Roosevelt. Also critical of the F-LP. No editor named.

MHS holdings: Jan. 1939

235. *Minnesota Bulletin.* Minneapolis: Socialist Party of Minnesota, 1918(?)–1919. Frequency unknown.

Paper reported Socialist party news and debates over tactics and strategies. The final issue covered the 1919 Chicago convention that formalized the party's split into Socialist and Communist parties. No editor named.

MHS holdings: 1:5 (Nov. 1918)– (?) (Sept. 1919) (Note: November issue on microfilm with *New Times*)

236. *Naisten Viiri* (Women's Banner). Yonkers, N.Y.: Finnish Federation, Inc., 1936–78. Weekly. In Finnish. (IHRC)

Continued *Työläisnainen* (Working Woman) in 1936. Closely connected to the Communist *Työmies* and later *Työmies-Eteenpäin*, the paper carried articles on housekeeping, health, cooking, and nutrition for Finnish women. Editors included Emma Mattila, Emma Tuominen, and Helen Kruth-Leiviska. Ceased in 1978 for financial reasons arising out of declining readership.

IHRC holdings: 1952–76

237. *New Times.* Minneapolis: Workers Pub. Co., 1910–19. Weekly.

Succeeded *New Commonwealth*. Edited by Alexis Georgian. The paper was for a few years the only English-language Socialist journal in Minnesota. It featured educational and theoretical pieces about the merits of Socialism, but it also provided heavy coverage of Minneapolis municipal affairs, in particular the corruption and vice in the police department. In 1918 it lost its second-class mailing permit and eventually ceased publication.

MHS holdings: 1:11 (Nov. 25, 1910)–8:22 (Jan. 1919)

238. *Northwest Communist.* Minneapolis: Communist Party of Minnesota, 1938(?)–(?). Frequency unknown.

Paper offered the Communist perspective on the "burning social issues of interest to the people of the Northwest." No editor named.

MHS holdings: 1:2 (Mar. 1938)

239. *Ny Tid* (New Times). Minneapolis: Lauritz Stavnheim, 1907–09. Monthly. In Norwegian.

Continued the short-lived Democratic *Politiken,* which had succeeded *Nye Normanden.* Lauritz Stavnheim regained control of the paper from its Democratic affiliation in 1907 and reinstated its original Socialist viewpoint. Paper ceased in 1909.
MHS holdings: 1:1 (Nov. 1907)–2:8 (June 1909)

240. *Nye Normanden* (New Norwegian). Minneapolis: Foss and Lund Pub. Co., 1894–1904. Weekly. In Norwegian.

A. A. Foss and Ed Lund founded the paper in Moorhead and moved it to Minneapolis in 1894. Editors included H. A. Foss, Olav Kringen, Emil Mengshoel, and Lauritz Stavnheim. Originally an anticapitalist, populist paper, under the editorship of Stavnheim it assumed a Socialist viewpoint. The paper was purchased by a Democratic politician in 1904, its title was changed to *Politiken,* and it was briefly associated with the Democratic party. In 1905, Stavnheim regained control of the paper, reestablished its Socialist stance, and changed its name to *Ny Tid.*
MHS holdings: Oct. 29, 1895–Sept. 14, 1897, Jan. 2, 1900–Dec. 24, 1901

241. *Referendum.* Faribault: Socialist Labor Party, 1899–1916(?). Weekly.

Edited by Ed Bosky and managed briefly by E. B. Ford. The paper was an organ of the Socialist Labor party, allied strongly with the IWW. It carried regular features and news from around the world as it related to the evils of capitalism. Much space devoted to differentiating its party from the Socialist party ("the fake SP"). In 1914 the Minnesota Socialist Labor party changed its name to the Industrial Labor party, but the paper used both names.
MHS holdings: 6:2 (June 24, 1911)–11:34 (Dec. 30, 1916)

242. *Representative.* Minneapolis: Representative Pub. Co., 1894(?)–1901. Weekly.

Edited by Ignatius Donnelly. The paper began as the "official journal of the State Farmer's Alliance and an Advocate of People's party principles" and carried general news and regular features. Editorials attacked American and European imperialism and called for public ownership of the railways. E. A. Twitchell took over the editorship after Donnelly's death in 1901 and allied the paper with the Socialist party. Shortly thereafter the paper ceased publication.
MHS holdings: 2:32 (Dec. 5, 1894)–9:20 (Nov. 28, 1901)

243. *Sosialisti.* Duluth: Socialist Pub. Co., 1914–16. Daily. In Finnish. (MHS and IHRC)

Editors included John Wiita. Midwestern radical Finns founded the paper after a split in the Finnish Socialist Federation between themselves, the midwest Socialist Työmies, and eastern Social Democrats. It came to support both the Socialist party and the IWW, but much of the paper was devoted to debates and conflicts between syndicalists and those who favored electoral party action. The paper provided heavy coverage of the 1916 miners' strike on the Iron Range, during which the editors supported the tactics of the IWW. The paper was continued by *Teollisuustyöläinen* (Industrial Worker) in 1916.
MHS holdings: 1:1 (June 11, 1914)–3:280 (Dec. 19, 1916)
IHRC holdings: 1:1 (June 11, 1914)–3:280 (Dec. 19, 1916)

244. *Sunday Worker.* Minneapolis: Communist Party, 1936(?)–(?). Weekly.

Paper educated its readers on Communist perspective of local politics. It was a Minnesota edition of the *Worker,* published by the Communist party in New York, and supported F-LP and profiled some of its candidates. No editor named.
MHS holdings: 2:23–24 (June 6–13, 1937)

245. *Teollisuustyöläinen* (Industrial Worker). Duluth: Socialist Pub. Co., 1916–17. Daily. In Finnish.

Continued *Sosialisti.* Editors included Leo Laukki, Fred Jaakkola, Taavi Heino, and William Risto. The editors changed the paper's name to reflect their increasing collaboration with the IWW. They were soon forced to change the name again after a minister of the Finnish Unitarian church sued them for libel. Continued by *Industrialisti* in 1917.
MHS holdings: 3:298–306 (Dec. 20–30, 1916)

246. *Truth.* Duluth: Duluth Cooperative Society, 1917–19; West End Labor Assn., 1919–23. Weekly.

Editors included William E. Reynolds, W. E. Towne, Jack Carney, J. O. Bentall, and Bertha Van Hove. Paper succeeded *Labor Leader.* It was founded by

Scandinavian branches of the Socialist party and was the official organ of the party in Duluth and Superior (until Sept. 1918) and of the Communist Labor party in the United States (after Sept. 1919). Initially the paper reported local, national, and women's suffrage news and featured regular columns and advertising, as its predecessor had. Jack Carney became editor in 1918 and shifted the paper's focus to international events. After 1919 the paper became primarily an instrument of the national left wing of the Socialist party, devoting itself to national and international news. Under the editorship of J. O. Bentall, the paper grew to see the farmer as an ally and lent its support to the F-LP. Publication ceased in 1923 due to financing troubles and possibly to the founding of the *Daily Worker*. MHS holdings: 1:1 (Oct. 19, 1917)–no. 301 (Apr. 13, 1923)

247. *Two Harbors Socialist.* Two Harbors: Socialist Party of Two Harbors, 1913–18. Weekly.

Edited by Juls J. Anderson and Louis Rose. Paper was primarily a local newspaper, carrying news of fraternal organizations, trade unions, city council meetings, and comings and goings of residents. The editors also published national news from the Socialist press, editorials by Eugene Debs and Scott Nearing, and speeches of other Socialists. Paper supported strikes, including 1916 miners' strike, woman suffrage, and Socialist candidates. It opposed U.S. entry into World War I. Succeeded by *Lake County Chronicle* in 1918.
MHS holdings: 3:1 (Feb. 13, 1915)–6:25 (July 26, 1918)

248. *Työläisnainen* (Working Woman). Superior: Työmies Pub. Co., 1930; Brooklyn, N.Y.: Finnish Federation, Inc., 1932–36. Weekly. In Finnish. (IHRC)

Continued *Toveritar* (Woman Comrade), which had been published by the Finnish Socialist Federation in Astoria, Oreg. Affiliated with the midwest district of the Finnish Socialist Federation, *Työläisnainen* presented the Communist position on issues to women, discussed women's issues from a Communist point of view, and carried articles on housekeeping, cooking, nutrition, and health. Evi Suvanto served as editor. Continued by *Naisten Viiri* (Women's Banner) in 1936.
IHRC holdings: Oct. 1930–Nov. 1931

249. *Työmies* (The Worker). Superior: Työmies Pub. Co.,

1903–50. Daily and weekly. In Finnish. (MHS and IHRC)

Began publication in Hancock, Mich., and moved to Superior in 1914. The paper was an organ of the midwest district of the Finnish Socialist Federation. During the split in the Socialist party, the newspaper supported the left-wing position, favored recognition of the Third International, and eventually became the Finnish-language organ of the Communist party in the Midwest. Its editors included Vihtori Kosonen, Leo Laukki, George Halonen, Richard Pesola, and Leo Mattson. In 1950 the New York-based *Eteenpäin* merged with *Työmies* to become *Työmies-Eteenpäin*, which is still published.
MHS holdings: Apr. 2–July 7, 1917, Jan. 3, 1924–Dec. 31, 1941, Jan. 1–Sept. 30, 1943, July 5, 6, 10, 1950
IHRC holdings: 1903–50 (Note: Issues missing for 1907)

250. *Työmies-Eteenpäin* (Worker-Forward). Superior: Työmies, 1950–present. Daily and three times a week. In Finnish.

Formed by merger of Superior's *Työmies* and the New York-based *Eteenpäin* in 1950.
MHS holdings: Aug. 17, 1950–present

251. *Työväen Osuustoimintalehti* (Workers' Co-operative Journal). Superior: Central Co-op Exchange, 1930–65. Weekly. In Finnish, some English. (IHRC)

Featured articles promoting the cooperative movement, but it also contained sections for farmers, working women, and youth on topics ranging from science and technology to literature. Editors included Henry Koski, George Halonen, Martti Larni, and Carl E. Davidson. Preceded by the *Osuustoimintan Tiedonantaja* (Newsletter). (Note: Issues at IHRC)
IHRC holdings: 1930–65

252. *United Action.* Minneapolis: Northwest Workers and Farmers Educational Assn., 1935–(?). Semimonthly.

Paper was an organ of the Communist party. Carried some national and world news but focused primarily on educating its readership on Communist perspective of local politics. Also featured two regular columns ("Pavement Pete Says" and "Jenny and Her Neighbors") about the foibles and evils of capitalism. No editor named.
MHS holdings: 1 (Aug. 1, 1935)–(Aug. 20, 1936)

253. *Uusi Kotimaa* (New Homeland). New York Mills: Peoples Voice Cooperative Pub. Co., 1923–34. Three times a week and weekly. In Finnish. (MHS and IHRC)

The paper was bought from the Nonpartisan League in 1919 by the Peoples Voice Cooperative Pub. Co., which had ties to the left wing of the Finnish Socialist Federation. It eventually became an organ of the Communist party. Editors included K. E. Heikkinen and Leo Mattson. In 1931 the paper moved to Superior where it was published by Työmies Pub. Co. It was discontinued in 1934.

MHS holdings: Jan. 16, 1919–Apr. 25, 1931
IHRC holdings: 1929–30, 1932–34

LABOR NEWSPAPERS

254. *American Constitution.* Minneapolis: Lewis Harthill, 1924–25(?). Weekly.

Edited by Lewis Harthill; Ralph Van Lear was vice-president and business manager. An anti-Communist paper that supported the AFL.

MHS holdings: 2:18 (Dec. 4, 1925)

255. *Arbeidsmanden* (The Worker). Fertile and Crookston: J. P. Bakken, 1900–05. Monthly. In Norwegian.

Edited by J. P. Bakken. The paper featured radical viewpoints on labor and politics.

MHS holdings: May 11, 1900–May 29, 1901

256. *Guild Striker.* Duluth: Lake Superior Newspaper Guild, 1938. Daily.

Edited by the "strikers themselves," guildsmen who were striking against the *Duluth Herald and News-Tribune.* The paper was initially a strike bulletin but quickly began to cover local news, claiming to be "your only local newspaper." The Apr. 8 issue was entitled *Duluth Guildsman,* but with the Apr. 9 issue the title became *Guild Daily,* which it remained until the strike was settled and the paper ceased publication in May 1938.

MHS holdings: 1:1–45 (Apr. 4–May 25, 1938)

257. *IUE Honeywell News.* Minneapolis: Local 1145 of the International Union of Electrical, Radio, and Machine Workers, 1945(?)–51(?). Monthly.

Began as the *UE Honeywell News* in 1945 but changed its name in 1949 when the IUE was organized. Paper covered activities and news of union members, as well as official union news. Paper was strongly anti-Com-

munist and carried many stories attacking the union's rival, the CIO's United Electrical Workers' Union. No editor named.

MHS holdings: 2:2 (Feb. 14, 1946)–3:11 (Aug. 14, 1947), Mar. 1950–Jan. 1951

258. *Independents.* Minneapolis: Independent Railroad Shops Assn., 1924–?. Frequency unknown.

Edited by H. B. Hill. Paper covered union news, activities, and internal affairs. Also reported on strikes.

MHS holdings: 1:1–5 (Oct. 15, 1924–Mar. 31, 1925)

259. *Industrial Organizer.* Minneapolis: Motor Transport and Allied Workers Industrial Union, Local 544 (CIO), 1941–42. Weekly.

Edited by Miles Dunne. Formed when Local 544 split into CIO 544 and the more moderate AFL 544. Paper vowed "to carry on the militant labor traditions of its honorable predecessor." It covered national CIO news and regularly criticized the AFL. Most of its pages were devoted to certification elections among furniture transport drivers and the trial of 29 leaders of the Local 544-CIO and the Socialist Workers' party indicted under the Smith Act. As the trial progressed, the paper provided day-by-day coverage and reflected on different theories about the principals and reasons behind the indictments. The publication ceased in 1942 due to lack of funds.

MHS holdings: 1:1–23 (July 17–Dec. 20, 1941), Feb. 3, 1942, May 16, 1942

260. *Labor World.* Duluth, 1896–present. Frequency varied.

Labor World was published as an independent newspaper until 1933, when it was bought by the Duluth Federated Trades Assembly; from 1935 to the present, it has been published by the Labor World Pub. Co. and allied strongly with the Trades Assembly. The paper was founded in 1896 by feminist and union organizer, Sabrie G. Akin. Under Akin's guidance, the paper was sympathetic to the Socialist cause, even as it allied itself with the Minnesota Federation of Labor and the Trades Assembly. When Akin died in 1900, William McEwen of the Duluth Federated Trades Assembly took over the paper, which remained independent and reported both sides of the conflict between the AFL and more militant labor activism. Throughout the 1920s, however, the paper opposed any organized labor movement outside the AFL. After 1933 it never regained the radicalism of its founding days, but it remained the voice of labor in Duluth and Superior.

MHS holdings: 1:1 (Apr. 11, 1896–Feb. 13, 1897), Mar. 3, 1900–present

261. *Lake County Chronicle.* Two Harbors: People's Pub. Co., 1918–30. Weekly.

Succeeded *Two Harbors Socialist.* Editors included Louis Rose and Clarence Hillman, who assumed editorship in 1919. A supporter of the Republican party, Hillman turned the paper away from its Socialist roots, believing that the previous "partisanship" of the paper was not in the community's best interests. He hoped to make the paper into a community labor paper, dependent upon subscriptions and advertisements from workers and small businesses. Succeeded by *Two Harbors Chronicle* in 1930.

MHS holdings: 6:35 (Oct. 4, 1918)–17:31 (July 31, 1930)

262. *Midwest Labor.* Duluth: Midwest District Council 12 of the International Woodworkers of America, 1937–40; Midwest Labor, Inc., 1940–44. Weekly.

Editors included S. K. Davis, P. R. McGraw, Irene Paull, and Ray Munson. Paper succeeded the *Timber Worker.* Under this title, the paper broadened its coverage to include news of the mines, farms, progressive AFL unions, and CIO unions in Minnesota, Wisconsin, and Michigan. It gradually evolved into a statewide CIO newspaper. The paper continued to carry the poems and stories of Calamity Jane (Irene Paull), as well as several other regular columns. It included a relatively small amount of political and electoral news when compared to other union papers. Most of its focus was on the CIO and the union movement. The paper did not disguise the existence of Communists in the CIO and vigorously opposed red-baiting; however, it was not a mouthpiece for the Communist movement. Succeeded by *Minnesota Labor* in 1944.

MHS holdings: 1:20 (Aug. 13, 1937)–8:1 (Feb. 11, 1944)

263. *Minneapolis Labor Review.* Minneapolis: Trades and Labor Assembly of Minneapolis and Hennepin County; Minneapolis Building Trades Council; International Assn. of Machinists District 48; Teamsters Joint Council 23, 1907–present. Weekly.

Succeeded *Employer and Employee,* a monthly magazine. Editors included John P. Kennedy, N. C. O'Connor, and Robley D. Cramer. The paper reported on labor legislation, union news, strikes, the Citizens Alliance, and boycotts, as well national and international news as it related to organized labor. It featured stories on poverty and working conditions in the state. The paper occasionally carried columns for women, concerning health, birth control, and women's role in the labor force, as well as homemaking tips. When covering Socialist and Communist activities, the paper took a more moderate editorial position. At various times, the paper supported municipal ownership of utilities, F-L associations, and an industrial union structure for the AFL. It gave heavy and favorable coverage to the 1934 truckers' strike and to the activities of the Workers' Alliance on behalf of the unemployed. By 1942, however, there was little, if any, coverage of radical activities. There was also no coverage of the F-LP's merger with the Democratic party, although the paper enthusiastically endorsed Hubert Humphrey for Minneapolis mayor in 1943.

MHS holdings: 1:1 (Apr. 4, 1907)–present

264. *Minnesota CIO Labor.* Minneapolis: Minnesota State CIO Council, 1947–56(?). Weekly.

Editors included Raymond Munson, Rodney Jacobson, and Emil Kreig. Succeeded *Minnesota Labor* as the official organ of Minnesota CIO unions. Like its predecessors, the paper focused on the news and activities of CIO unions, although it also reported some local and national news. In 1948 it began to report favorably on the expulsion of Communists from the CIO, a purge that continued to receive extensive coverage well into 1950.

MHS holdings: 9:48 (Jan. 24, 1947)–8:21(?)(Nov. 2, 1956) (Note: On microfilm with *Minnesota Labor*)

265. *Minnesota Labor.* Minneapolis: Minnesota State CIO Council, 1944–47. Weekly.

Editors included George Kelley, Leonard Lageman, John Kykyri, and Raymond Munson. Succeeded *Midwest Labor* to become the official organ of the CIO in Minnesota, focusing on the news and activities of CIO unions. It continued to highlight cooperation among the AFL, CIO, and railroad brotherhoods, even as it reported on the tensions among the leadership of these groups. It also reported on national and state legislation and featured stories about housing discrimination, wage disparity between men and women, racial prejudice in the

Farmer-Labor newspapers had many uses, including decorating a speakers platform about 1935. The headline in this July issue of the Minnesota Leader *reads, "F-L Launches Vast Rural Electric Plan on Cooperative Public Ownership Basis."*

labor movement, and the Ku Klux Klan. In 1945 a cartoon history of the labor movement illustrated how racial and religious intolerance divided and weakened the movement. Coverage of the unions in Duluth and on the Iron Range remained strong. Irene Paull and Meridel Le Sueur contributed regularly. Succeeded by *Minnesota CIO Labor* in 1947.
MHS holdings: 8:2 (Feb. 18, 1944)–9:47 (Jan. 17, 1947)

266. *Minnesota Teamster.* Minneapolis: Teamsters Joint Council 32, 1941–44. Weekly.

Continued in part the *Northwest Organizer.* Founded when Teamsters' Local 544 split into AFL 544 and CIO 544. Paper spoke for the International Brotherhood of Teamsters, Chauffers, Warehousemen and Helpers of America, Local 544 (AFL). Paper covered union news, mostly centered on the internal troubles of Local 544. For all of its attacks on the CIO,

however, the paper advocated a united front between the AFL and the CIO. Editors included Lester Hunt, Raymond Leheney, and Martin Quigley. Succeeded in 1944 by the *Northwest Teamster.*
MHS holdings: 1:1 (July 3, 1941)–10:12 (Dec. 28, 1944)

267. *Minnesota Union Advocate.* St. Paul: Minnesota State Federation of Labor; St. Paul Trades and Labor Assembly, 1897–present. Weekly.

Editors included P. J. Geraghty, Cornelius Guiney, William Mahoney, and A. B. Lockhart. The paper chronicled labor legislation, strikes, the unionization of unorganized workers, and news from local and statewide unions. It also featured, at various times, short stories, religious columns, and women's pages. While the first issues were devoted to the "toiling masses," the paper made it clear that it would

not be a forum for revolutionaries and pursued a nonpartisan stance. It supported Debs and public ownership of railways but was often critical of the Socialist party, especially its opposition to World War I. Under Mahoney's editorship, 1923–32, the paper encouraged and chronicled the formation of F-L associations and stood somewhat to the left of the more moderate positions of the AFL. The paper supported the New Deal, Roosevelt, and later, World War II, although it offered its pages for debates about these issues. What was ignored over the years of its publication is noteworthy, however. There was little coverage of either the 1934 truckers' strike or the turbulent timber workers' strike and no coverage of the 1941 sedition trial involving 18 former leaders of Local 574/544. There was also no mention of the 1943 merger of the F-LP with the Democratic party. In 1965 became the *Union Advocate*.
MHS holdings: 1:1 (Jan. 22, 1897)–present

268. *Northwest Organizer*. Minneapolis: Northwest Labor Unity Conference, 1935–36; Minneapolis Teamsters' Joint Council, 1936–41. Weekly.
Editors included Pat Corcoran, Farrell Dobbs, Jack Smith, and Miles Dunne. Succeeded the *Organizer*. The paper served the militant labor movement of the Upper Midwest and was not strictly connected to one particular party. Most of its space was devoted to the activities of Teamsters Local 574 (later 544) and its various sections. The paper both chronicled and aided Local 574/544's successful efforts to unionize workers and support strikes. Its pages also carried the heated debates and conflicts surrounding tactics and philosophies of different organizations, such as the AFL, the Communist party, the Socialist Workers party, the F-LP, and the CIO. The paper ceased publication in 1941 following Local 544's split into CIO 544 and AFL 544 and was replaced by the *Industrial Organizer* (CIO 544) and *Minnesota Teamster* (AFL 544).
MHS holdings: 1:1 (Apr. 16, 1935)–7:13(July 10, 1941)

269. *Organizer*. Minneapolis: Teamsters' Local 574 (General Drivers and Helpers Union), 1934. Weekly and daily.
Strike bulletin of the General Drivers and Helpers Union during the Minneapolis truck drivers' strike of 1934. Edited by Farrell Dobbs. The bulletin chronicled the events and grievances leading up to the strike, provided daily coverage of the strike when

it began in July, and continued with weekly coverage of the union after the strike was settled. The bulletin also featured two regular columns: "The National Picket Line," devoted to labor developments around the country, and "Labor Looks at the Press," reprints of stories and editorials from the mainstream press, with commentary. Herbert Solow contributed often to the bulletin. Succeeded by the *Northwest Organizer* in 1935.
MHS holdings: 1:1–48 (June 25–Oct. 17, 1934)

270. *People's Press*. Philadelphia: People's Press, Inc., 1935(?)–38(?). Weekly.
Issued by Locals 1138, 1139, 1140, 1142, and 1143 of the United Electrical, Radio and Machine Workers of America (CIO). Paper was the Minneapolis edition of a national union publication; however, it was edited in Minneapolis by Hilliard Smith. It contained mostly national union news, carried a women's page, and featured many stories about the CIO and John L. Lewis.
MHS holdings: 4:2–9 (Nov. 12–Dec. 31, 1938)

271. *Range Labor News*. Virginia: John Edman, 1919(?)–21(?). Weekly.
Affiliated with the AFL. It carried the news of AFL locals on the Iron Range and featured stories about low wages, justice for the laboring classes, and the right to strike. Also printed news from the American Legion and Rotary Club, as well as a weekly adventure story.
MHS holdings: 3:39–47 (Oct. 21–Dec. 30, 1921)

272. *Striker's News*. Hibbing: Strikers of the Mesabi Range, 1916. Irregular.
Official bulletin of the striking iron ore workers on the Mesabi Range. Edited by "the strikers themselves."
MHS holdings: Aug. 4–Sept. 22, 1916

273. *Timber Worker*. Duluth: Timber Workers' Union Local 2776, 1937. Weekly.
Edited by S. K. Davis. Paper covered union activities, strikes, and organizing drives in Minnesota, Wisconsin, and Michigan. Reported favorably on the activities of Chester Watson and the Workers' Alliance and supported Governor Elmer Benson and the F-LP. Carried poems and stories by Irene Paull, alias Calamity Jane and Lumberjack Sue. Succeeded by *Midwest Labor* in Aug. 1937.

MHS holdings: 1:1–19 (Apr. 2–Aug. 6, 1937)
(Note: On microfilm with *Midwest Labor*)

274. *Two Harbors Chronicle.* Two Harbors: Warren Hillman, 1930–(?). Weekly.

Editors included C. M. Hillman and G. E. Morrison. Succeeded *Lake County Chronicle.* The paper carried local news and featured regular columns. G. E. Morrison, a staunch Farmer-Laborite, assumed the editorship, 1931–32, and brought a more progressive tone to the paper. In 1932 the more conservative Hillman resumed editorship.
MHS holdings: 17:32 (Aug. 7, 1930)–30:52 (Dec. 30, 1943)

275. *Unionist.* Austin: Independent Union of All Workers, 1935–37; Packinghouse Workers Organizing Committee, 1937–40; Local 9 (United Packinghouse Workers of America), 1940–79; Local P-9 of the United Food and Commercial Workers, 1979–present. Weekly.

Editors included Carl Nilson and Svend Godfredsen. Paper began as organ of the IUAW and maintained its militant tone into the early 1940s, containing within its pages the diverse voices of Communists, Trotskyists, Socialists, and trade unionists. Paper covered CIO national news and activities and meetings of locals, as well as some general news. Paper carried many regular columns of political commentary, hunting and fishing tips, movie reviews, and cartoons.
MHS holdings: Sept. 27, 1940–Nov. 28, 1986

276. *Whoozit Sandwich.* Minneapolis: Minneapolis Typographical Union 42, 1944–45. Monthly.

Edited by union members. Paper previously reported union sporting news, but in 1944 it resumed publication as a newsletter for the union members in the armed forces. The Minneapolis Star Journal Tribune Co. allowed the printers to use its press for the publication, which is fairly elaborate for a newsletter. Reported personal news, such as births, weddings, and family events, rather than official union news. Featured letters and columns from members overseas. Ceased publication at the end of World War II.
MHS holdings: 4:1 (May 1944)–5:5 (Sept. 1945)

FARMER-LABOR NEWSPAPERS

277. *Albert Lea Freeborn Patriot.* Albert Lea: Ostby & Ostby, 1935?–? Weekly.

Edited by Roger B. Ostby. Paper stood solidly behind the F-LP and reported state political news, with commentary. It also covered some local news and featured regular columns, including Susie Stageberg's "As a Woman Sees It," originally published in the *Minnesota Leader.* Slogan was "Eat more butter—Drink more milk."
MHS holdings: May 27, Aug. 5, Oct. 28, 1938

278. *Farm Holiday News.* St. Paul: Farm Holiday Pub. Co., 1933–34; Marissa, Ill.: Farm Holiday Pub. Co., 1934–35; Ames, Iowa: Farm Holiday Pub. Co., 1935–36. Monthly and semimonthly.

Issued by the National Farm Holiday Assn. Editors included Milo Reno, A. F. Lockhart, H. R. Gross, and Dale Kramer. Paper covered primarily farm issues (product prices, mortgages, farm strikes) and international and national news as it related to farmers. Paper also featured regular columns of political commentary and cartoons. Paper supported Floyd B. Olson but criticized Roosevelt. It was largely a vehicle for the views of Milo Reno, the president of the association. The paper merged with the *Farmers' National Weekly* in 1936 to form the *National Farm Holiday News.*
MHS holdings: Feb. 20, 1933–Jan. 1934

279. *Farmer-Labor Advocate.* St. Paul: Farmer-Labor Educational Committee, 1923–27. Weekly.

Edited by W. E. Quigley; business manager, William Mahoney. The paper reported state news as it related to the F-LP and carried regular columns of political commentary, party news, and educational tidbits. Paper was concerned about the presence of Communists in the F-LP and published several anti-Communist articles. Ceased in 1927 when F-L conference endorsed a monthly magazine. Subscribers were offered the *Minnesota Union Advocate* to complete their subscriptions.
MHS holdings: Feb. 9, 1923–Feb. 1, 1927

280. *Farmer-Labor Leader.* St. Paul: Minnesota Farmer-Labor Assn., 1930–34. Semimonthly.

Editors included Henry Teigan and H. G. Creel. Paper covered official F-LP news, conventions, election campaigns, and the activities of Floyd B. Olson. It carried a regular women's column by Susie Stageberg and articles by Scott Nearing, Walfrid Engdahl, and O. M. Thomason. The paper sought to "rescue the government from the control of the privileged few and make it function for the use and benefit of all by abolishing monopoly in every form." It pushed for unemployment insurance, promoted public ownership, and boosted co-ops. National politics appeared only as it related to the formation of a national F-LP. However, the paper's masthead carried the blue eagle of the National Recovery Act. Succeeded in 1935 by a new *Minnesota Leader*.

MHS holdings: 1:1 (Jan. 1, 1930)–5:24 (Dec. 30, 1934)

281. *Farmer-Labor Progressive*. St. Paul: Farmer-Labor Political Federation and League for Independent Political Action, 1934–? Monthly.

Edited by Howard Y. Williams, executive secretary of the League for Independent Political Action. The paper was intended to pave the way for a national F-LP. It advocated socialist ideas, connecting them to the democratic principles of American thought and dissociating them from Communist ideas. Paper carried general news as it related to its purposes, as well as regular columns reviewing recent political books and discussing the disparity of wealth in the U.S.

MHS holdings: 1:1 (Mar. 21, 1939)–2:3 (Mar. 1941) (Note: Some issues missing)

282. *Farmers' National Weekly*. Washington, D.C.: Farmers National Committee for Action, 1933; Chicago, Ill.: Farmers National Educational Assn., 1934–35; Minneapolis: Farmers National Educational Assn., 1935–36. Weekly.

Editors included Rob F. Hall and Eric Bert; business managers, John Miller and Walter Harju. Paper reported national and international news as it related to farm issues. It carried regular columns of political commentary, humor, poetry, and human interest, including Lem Harris's column on farm conditions in the Soviet Union and Katharine Harris's full-page features on "The Farm Woman." Initially the paper leaned toward a Communist viewpoint and criticized the reformist efforts of the National Farm Holiday Assn., President Roosevelt, and the New Deal. Gradually, however, the paper came to support the formation of a national F-LP and joined ranks with other farmers' organizations. In 1936 the paper merged with the *Farm Holiday News* to form the *National Farm Holiday News*.

MHS holdings: 1:1 (Jan. 30, 1933)–3:25 (Aug. 21, 1936)

283. *Minnesota Daily Star*. Minneapolis: Northwest Pub. Co., 1920–(?). Daily.

Edited by Herbert Gaston; vice-president, Thomas Van Lear. The paper, like other dailies, carried international and national news, as well as sports, business, and entertainment sections. Its editorial pages, however, revealed its affiliation with the Working People's NPL. It promoted public ownership of utilities and railroads and the principles of the league. It supported Eugene Debs during his imprisonment. Bankruptcy in 1924 resulted in the paper's sale to a team of new owners with close ties to big business. Succeeded by the *Minneapolis Daily Star*.

MHS holdings: 1:1 (Aug. 19, 1920)–6:114 (June 30, 1924)

284. *Minnesota Leader*. St. Paul: National Nonpartisan League in Minnesota, 1918–20; Minneapolis: National Nonpartisan League in Minnesota, 1920–24. Weekly and semimonthly.

Editors included Oliver S. Morris, A. B. Gilbert, and O. M. Thomason. The paper covered farm conditions, legislation, and political news as it related to farmers, as well as to A. C. Townley. It carried some news about organized labor and cartoons about farmer-labor alliances. The paper noted NPL club meetings and featured a regular column devoted to the women's NPL clubs, written by Kate Gregg and, later, Susie Stageberg. According to the reports, the women's clubs and the statewide conventions they held were a lively part of the NPL during its last years. The paper was friendly toward Socialism and opposed red-baiting until 1924, when a series of anti-Communist editorials appeared. The paper was skeptical about the formation of a F-LP and advocated working within the existing parties to make them more responsive to workers and farmers. It urged a boycott of the 1924 F-LP convention, which had been promoted by William Mahoney, head of the Working People's NPL. By 1924 the number of NPL members had dropped considerably (many turning to the new F-LP), and in November the paper admitted that not much was left of the farmers' movement in the state. The paper was succeeded in 1924 by a new *Minnesota Leader*, which was published in Olivia.

MHS holdings: 1:1 (Feb. 16, 1918)–7:10 (Nov. 15, 1924)

285. *Minnesota Leader*. Olivia: Nonpartisan League in Minnesota, 1925–26. Monthly.

Edited by H. E. Marsh; P. J. Gleason, business manager. Succeeded the old *Minnesota Leader*. Paper moved to Olivia as part of the NPL's reorganization into a more decentralized, regional organization. The first editorial promised to carry on the editorial policy of the former paper and went on to express dissatisfaction with the "farmer-labor experiment." Much of the paper was devoted to reinvigorating the dying organization. Paper moved back to Minneapolis in 1926.

MHS holdings: 7:11 (Jan. 1, 1925)–9:5 (May 29, 1926)

286. *Minnesota Leader*. Minneapolis: Minnesota Nonpartisan League, 1926–27; Minnesota Leader Pub. Co., 1927–32. Irregular.

Editors included Tom Davis. Succeeded the Olivia *Minnesota Leader* but bore little resemblance to it. Published sporadically. Each issue appears to be devoted to a single issue—sugar-beet growers or the Tom Davis campaign for governor, for instance. Under the editorship of Tom Davis in 1930, the paper became an organ of the Progressive Republican party, and later, with the last issue, the Independent Progressive party.

MHS holdings: 9:6 (June 19, 1926)–11:2 (June 12, 1932) (Note: Some issues missing)

287. *Minnesota Leader*. St. Paul: Minnesota Farmer-Labor Assn., 1935–49. Weekly.

Succeeded the *Farmer-Labor Leader*. Editors included Henry Teigan, Abe I. Harris, and William Mahoney. The paper changed its name to broaden its scope and readership. Paper covered general international and national news, as well as the news and activities of the F-LP. It continued to carry Susie Stageberg's column, "As a Woman Sees It." The paper printed many articles about Communist activity in the F-LP, which it neither endorsed nor denounced, but was critical of red-baiting. The paper initially opposed intervention in World War II; however, once the war began, it became an enthusiastic supporter. Similarly, it did not originally approve of a merger with the Democratic party; however, by 1942 the paper assented to the merger.

MHS holdings: 6:1 (Jan. 5, 1935)–20:1 (Mar. 1, 1949)

288. *National Farm Holiday News*. Minneapolis: National Farm Holiday News, Inc., 1936–37. Weekly.

Edited by Dale Kramer. Succeeded both *Farm Hol-iday News* and *Farmers' National Weekly*, which merger was the result of farm organizations' efforts to unify and strengthen their fight against a common enemy. The paper supported and worked for the F-LP, while continuing to stand by the Farm Holiday program. The paper carried national and international news, offered commentary on national issues, and reported on farm matters. It also featured many regular columns of political opinion, humor, letters, and puzzles, including a full-page feature, "Farm Women of Today." The paper ceased publication in 1937 in a further effort to consolidate and unify the farm movement. Subscribers were offered subscriptions to either the *Minnesota Leader* or *American Guardian* (Oklahoma City). Dale Kramer went to work for the *Minnesota Leader*.

MHS holdings: 1:1 (Aug. 28, 1936)–2:8 (Dec. 31, 1937)

289. *Our Time*. Minneapolis: Executive Committee of the Hennepin County Farmer-Labor Assn., 1939–(?). Monthly.

Paper carried internal news of the F-LP in Hennepin County, such as reports on F-L women's clubs and ward meetings.

MHS holdings: 1:1 (Mar. 21, 1939)–2:3 (Mar. 1941) (Note: Some issues missing)

290. *Ramsey County Guardian*. St. Paul: Minnesota Worker's Alliance, 1937(?)–(?). Irregular.

Edited by Kristin Svanum. Paper carried news of Worker's Alliance activities, meetings, and goals. Also reported on the plight of the unemployed. Enthusiastically supported the F-LP, President Roosevelt, and the New Deal.

MHS holdings: 2:1 (Oct. 11, 1930)–2:4 (Dec. 20, 1938)

291. *State News*. Minneapolis and St. Paul: Arthur Jacobs, 1929(?)–(?). Monthly.

Edited by Arthur Jacobs. The paper covered state electoral news relating to all parties. It also carried short stories, cartoons, and other regular columns. The paper spoke out against trusts and big business and generally supported candidates who did likewise, regardless of their party affiliation. By 1936, however, Jacobs had become a staunch Farmer-Laborite, endorsing only F-LP candidates and running regularly the speeches of Elmer Benson and

Henry Teigan. Ernest Lundeen wrote a monthly column called "What the national lawmakers are doing." By 1939, the paper had completely dropped its nonpartisan approach, endorsing the F-LP and attacking the Republicans.
MHS holdings: 2:8 (Mar. 1930)–10:5 (May 1939) (Note: Some issues missing)

292. *United Farmer.* New York Mills: United Farmers League, 1925–31. Monthly.

Paper was an organizing tool for the United Farmers League. It presented the league's critique of the banking system and reformist organizations (F-LP, co-ops, and farmers' unions). It opposed war preparedness, praised the USSR, reported on the Tom Mooney case, and mentioned lynchings in the South. Paper lost its second-class mailing permit in 1931 and ceased publication.
MHS holdings: Nov. 1930–July 1931

MISCELLANEOUS NEWSPAPERS

293. *Minnesota Progressive.* Minneapolis, [1920s?]. Frequency unknown.

Paper advocated the policies and principles of Robert M. La Follette and sought to be a literary digest of political thought for the Northwest. Paper was critical of trusts and corporations.
MHS holdings: June 1923

294. *Päivälehti* (Daily Journal). Duluth: Finnish Pub. Co., 1901–48. Daily. In Finnish. (IHRC)

Started in 1901 in Calumet, Mich., it was bought in 1914 and moved to Duluth. It served as the voice of the conservative Finnish business community, reported Finnish-American events, including labor news, and supported the Republican party through the 1920s. It was bought in 1940 by the social democratic Raivaaja Pub. Co. of Fitchburg, Mass. Editors included J. S. Ollila.
IHRC holdings: Jan. 1, 1908–Oct. 15, 1948 (Note: Some issues missing)

295. *Pink Sheet.* Minneapolis: H. A. Guilfoud, 1932(?)–(?). Weekly.

Paper claimed to be published "in the interests of fair play for the underdog" and had no explicit political ties. Paper primarily contained criticisms of the Dayton, Jaffrey, and Piper families for their perceived exemption from society's morals and laws.
MHS holdings: June 17, 1932

Oral Histories

The oral history interviews included here were produced by six different projects, including the 20th-Century Radicalism in Minnesota Project. There is also a section of miscellaneous interviews. The interviews are arranged below in seven sections. Within each group, the entries are listed alphabetically by surname of the person interviewed. Several individuals appear as interviewees in more than one section. Unless otherwise noted, all of the recorded interviews and their transcripts, if they have been made, are available in the Sound and Visual Collection of the Minnesota Historical Society; a few are located at regional historical centers in Duluth (Duluth), Marshall (Southwest), Moorhead (Moorhead), Morris (Rwest central), or Mankato (OMankato).

The MHS interviews are accessible through the Sound and Visual Collection card catalog or the Oral History Collection notebooks in the Research Center.

20TH-CENTURY RADICALISM IN MINNESOTA

Most of the interviews listed below were conducted for the 20th-Century Radicalism in Minnesota Project by Carl Ross, Sal Salerno, Peter Rachleff, Susanna Frenkel, Virginia Hyvärinen, Hyman Berman, Linda Schloff, and others between 1986 and 1989. The project also collected and transcribed interviews that had been conducted earlier; these are also included.

296. Anderson, Jacob (1902–). 1977. 90 min. 23 p.
Anderson was born and raised in the Finnish community of northern Minnesota. He joined the IWW when he was 15 and the Communist party in 1928. He was a party organizer in Minnesota throughout the 1930s. He discusses Communist party education efforts, the farmers' hunger march, Minnesota logging, the cooperative movement in northern Minnesota, and Sacco and Vanzetti.
Interviewers: Steve Trimble and Tom O'Connell

297. Arnio, Arnold F. (Arnie) (1904–). 1987. 30 min. 9 p.
Arnio was born in Finland in 1904; his family immigrated to Minnesota's Iron Range shortly thereafter. He became involved in the labor movement on the range in the 1910s and 1920s. He recalls the 1916 miners' strike, his participation in the 1922 railway shopmen's strike in Duluth (for which he was blacklisted), and his later involvement with the United Steel Workers of America.
Interviewer: Carl Ross

298. Bester, Earl T. (1900–), with Joseph Paszak (1908–). 1980. 2 hrs. 30 p.
Bester played a key role in the Steel Workers Organizing Committee (CIO) and served as the Duluth/Iron Range district director of the United Steel Workers of America (USWA), 1952–65. Paszak was president of USWA Local 1210 and chair of the CIO Council in Duluth. The interview focuses on the years 1936–50, obstacles to organizing labor unions, the formation of the Duluth CIO Council, and the merger of the AFL and CIO in 1955. Bester also discusses the 1946 and 1948 congressional campaigns of John Blatnik. This interview was part of KUMD's Seniors Program at the University of Minnesota–Duluth and was transcribed and edited by the 20th-Century Radicalism in Minnesota Project.
Interviewer: Jean Johnson

299. Blatnik, Frank P. (1914–). 1989. 3 hrs., 45 min. 63 p.
Born in Chisholm, Blatnik was involved in the politically active South Slav community of Chisholm and was also a teacher for the WPA Workers Education Program in the 1940s. He discusses growing up in a Slovene family, boardinghouse life, the CIO-led organizing drive on the Iron Range, and the roots of his brother John Blatnik's political career and his role in it. Interview expands and supple-

ments his 1942 master's thesis, "Culture Conflict: A Study of the Slovenes in Chisholm, Minnesota."
Interviewer: Carl Ross

300. Boratko, Andre (1911–   ). 1988. 45 min. 6 p.
Boratko taught at the St. Paul School of Arts and was involved in the WPA Federal Art Project. He discusses his Czech family, his art training, the art he created for the WPA, and his murals at Milaca.
Interviewer: Sal Salerno

301. Borchardt, Arthur. 1976. 90 min. 30 p.
Borchardt farmed in Pine County from the early 1900s through the 1930s. He was active in the NPL and later aided in the development of the F-LP. Borchardt also served on the merger committee of the DFL. Interview focuses on farmers' associations and Communist party activities in Pine County.
Interviewers: Steve Trimble and Tom O'Connell

302. Broms, Wilbur S. (1912–   ). 1987. 3 hrs. 61 p.
Broms's family was involved with the Socialist party and later the Communist party. He discusses growing up in the St. Paul radical community in the 1920s and 1930s, his parents' activities in the Socialist party just before its split, and their subsequent support of the new Communist party. He recalls his experience in the Twin Cities Young Communist League in the 1930s and his service in World War II. He also touches on his career as a singer, first at local radical meetings and later with the Metropolitan Opera.
Interviewer: Carl Ross

303. Bruce, D(ouglas) Alan (1910–   ). 1988, 1989. 2 hrs. 20 p.
Interview focuses on Bruce's work as state director of WPA Worker Education Program in the 1940s. Discusses accusations of radicalism against the program and efforts of Communists and Trotskyists to influence the program. Also discusses the militant labor movement.
Interviewer: Carl Ross

304. Bruce, Elizabeth (Betty) Hoff (1913–   ). 1989. 2 hrs. 34 p.
Interview focuses on Bruce's social work at the North East Neighborhood House and the YWCA, both in Minneapolis, in the late 1930s and 1940s. Bruce conducted a program to find employment for Nisei women who wished to join their husbands in the Twin Cities and also directed the cultural activities section of the WPA Worker Education Program in Minneapolis in the 1930s. She describes the role of social-service organizations in community life.
Interviewer: Carl Ross

305. Carlson, Grace Holmes (1906–92). 1987. 3 hrs., 20 min. 48 p.
Carlson was the Socialist Workers party candidate for U.S. Senate in 1946, vice-president in 1948, and Congress in 1950. Along with other local Trotskyists, she was convicted in 1941 of violating the Smith Act and served a term in a federal prison. She describes growing up in the Irish community of St. Paul, her work in Minnesota as an organizer for the Socialist Workers party, the 1934 Minneapolis truck drivers' strike, and relations between Trotskyists and Socialists.
Interviewer: Carl Ross

306. Darcy, Sam (1905–   ). Undated. 2 hrs. 68 p.
Darcy was a high-ranking member in the Communist party, whose career in the party was ultimately hampered by his long-standing conflicts with Earl Browder, the general secretary. He served as the party's national educational director and Central Committee representative for the Minnesota-Wisconsin-Dakotas district, 1938–39. In this position, he became acquainted with Governor Elmer Benson and worked to explain the relationship between the Communist and F-L parties to both Communist leadership and red-baiting critics. He was expelled from the party in 1944. In this interview he discusses Minnesota and Communist party politics and puts the F-LP in international context.
Interviewer: Robb Mitchell

307. DeBoer, Harry (1905–91), Pauline DeBoer, and Jake Cooper (1916–90). 1988. 75 min., 60 min. 18 p., 15 p.
DeBoer was a paid organizer for the Teamsters. He was convicted in 1941 under the Smith Act of conspiring to overthrow the government. With the help of Pauline DeBoer, his wife, and Jake Cooper, a Chaska store owner involved in militant unionism, he discusses the truck drivers' strike of 1934, Trotskyists, the IWW, the Communist party, Ray Dunne, and Carl Skoglund.
Interviewers: Sal Salerno (first interview); Sal Salerno, Peter Rachleff, and Randy Furst (second interview)

308. DeMaio, Ernest (1908–   ). 1988. 3 hrs. 46 p.
DeMaio was a member of the Communist party and a left-wing trade unionist. He helped organize the United Electrical, Radio, and Machine Workers Union (UE) in 1936 and came to Chicago in 1940 as a regional director for the UE. DeMaio is associated with the successful organization of the UE in Minnesota. He was active in the 1948 election campaign that resulted in the expulsion of the UE and other left-wing unions from the CIO.
Interviewer: Carl Ross

309. Dizard, George (1917–   ). 1987. 2 hrs., 30 min. 36 p.
Dizard was born and raised in Duluth. In the 1930s, he was active in the Minnesota Youth Congress. Later he worked at the Duluth Diamond Caulk and Horseshoe Co. and organized an AFL local. Dizard became a major spokesperson for the left wing and for "Duluth's labor progressives" during the 1940s and 1950s. He discusses his involvement in the St. Louis County DFL party, Eighth District politics, and Henry Wallace's 1948 presidential campaign. Dizard married Rhoda Levine.
Interviewer: Carl Ross

310. Drill, Edwin G. (1910–   ). 1987. 2 hrs. 30 p.
Drill was born in Wisconsin and raised in Duluth. He became involved in the labor movement while working at Western Paint and Varnish Co. with Ernest Pearson. He discusses life in 1930s Duluth, his part in the organization of the Gas, Coke, and Chemical Workers Union local in Duluth, which he represented at the Duluth CIO Council, and left-wing leadership in organizing unions.
Interviewer: Carl Ross

311. Enestvedt, John (1906–   ). 1988. 60 min. 17 p.
Born and raised near Sacred Heart, Enestvedt was actively involved in the NPL, the Socialist Workers party, and the Farm Holiday Assn. He discusses these organizations and also his association with Farrell Dobbs.
Interviewer: Sal Salerno

312. Engdahl, Walfrid. 1972. 60 min. 7 p.
Engdahl, who was born in Sweden, immigrated to Minnesota in 1909 and became an organizer for the IWW. He served as editor of *Allarm*, 1917–18, a paper published by the Scandinavian Propaganda League of the IWW. In this radio interview, Engdahl discusses Swedish immigration and Scandinavian involvement in syndicalist activism.
Interviewer: Steven Benson for KUOM's *Minnesota's Lifestyles* sponsored by the University of Minnesota

313. Fine, Fred M. (1914–   ). 1988. 1 hr., 45 min. 25 p.
Fine grew up in a radical Jewish family in Chicago and early in his life became active in the Young Pioneers and later in the Young Communist League. Fine moved to Minnesota as a representative of the National Committee of the YCL and describes working with Carl Ross and other local youth activists, 1937–40. He also discusses Communist party tactics and strategy with regard to Minnesota politics.
Interviewer: Carl Ross

314. Flower, James H. (1906–86). 1977. 2 hrs. 31 p.
Flower grew up in rural Minnesota and became active in the labor movement after moving to Minneapolis in 1933. He discusses working and living conditions in Minnesota in the 1930s, the Unemployed Councils, the United Farmers' League, and Communist party politics.
Interviewers: Steve Trimble and Tom O'Connell

315. Foley, Alma Howe (1909–   ). 1988. 2 hrs., 45 min. 39 p.
Foley was born near Alden, Freeborn County, and in the 1930s became an activist for civil rights and the unemployed in Duluth and Minneapolis. She headed the state chapter of the International Labor Defense, 1935–40. She discusses the relationship between the International Labor Defense and the Communist party. Foley headed the state chapter of the American Committee for Protection of the Foreign Born, 1950–58. She relates her experiences with the committee as a publicly known and active Communist and being called to testify before the House Un-American Activities Committee. The interview also includes information on Tom Foley, her husband, an organizational secretary for the Communist party.
Interviewer: Carl Ross

316. Forester, Clarence M. (1915–   ). 1989. 1 hr., 45 min. 26 p.
Forester grew up on a farm in North Dakota. He recalls his experiences as a young radical in Superior and Minneapolis in the 1930s, his half-brothers Rudolph and Walter Harju, his service in Spain as

part of the Abraham Lincoln Brigade, and his subsequent experience as an artilleryman in Europe during World War II. He also discusses his activities in the radical Finnish community of North Minneapolis. Forester donated insignia from his Lincoln Brigade uniform to the Minnesota Historical Society (see no. 703).
Interviewer: Carl Ross

317. Fossum, Bernice (Bunny). 1988. 2 hrs. 42 p.
Bunny Fossum joined the Communist party in the 1930s and was active in the Twin Cities radical labor movement. She belonged to the Minneapolis Theatre Union, an amateur theatrical group. Syd Fossum, her husband, was a founder of the Artists' Union. She discusses the Twin Cities community of radical artists in the 1930s and early 1940s, her involvement in various strikes (Strutwear, WPA, and Miller's), the Spanish Loyalists in the Civil War, harassment by the FBI, and her husband's activities in the Artists' Union.
Interviewer: Sal Salerno

318. Fossum, Bernice (Bunny). 1978. 90 min. 29 p.
See above entry for biographical information. In this interview, Fossum discusses the Le Sueur family and WPA theater groups.
Interviewer: Steve Trimble

319. Freeman, Orville L. (1918–   ). 1988. 80 min. 36 p.
Freeman was a DFL governor of Minnesota, 1955–61. The interview focuses on Freeman's post-World War II political career, specifically his activities with the American Veterans Committee and as secretary and chair of the Minnesota DFL party during the early years of the Cold War. He also discusses the personal attempts of himself and his wife, Jane, to reconcile with her father, James Shields, a Progressive party activist who ran against Humphrey as an independent left-wing candidate in 1948.
Interviewers: Carl Ross and Hyman Berman

320. Friedman, Newton (1912–   ). 1988. 70 min. 20 p.
Friedman discusses his family's experiences as Jewish immigrants and radicals. He focuses on Samuel F. Friedman, his father, who was secretary of the Socialist party of Minnesota in 1919 during the split with the Communist party and who remained in the Socialist party after the split. The family moved to New York in 1931. Friedman moved to Duluth after World War II and practiced law, specializing in labor and civil-liberties cases. He also describes the activities of the Workmen's Circle, a radical Jewish organization (in which he was still active).
Interviewers: Carl Ross and Susanna Frenkel

321. Gates, Lillian. 1977. 60 min. 23 p.
Gates was deeply involved in Minnesota politics, 1935–37. She was Lieutenant-governor Hjalmar Petersen's secretary until Feb. 1937 when she resigned to work openly as a Communist. She was an insider in the F-LP and offers insight into Communist activity within the party, as well as the party's decline.
Interviewer: Hyman Berman

322. Geldman, Max (1905–89). 1988. 90 min. 15 p.
Geldman discusses his experiences as a young Trotskyist in the Minneapolis Young Communist League. The Trotskyist group was expelled from the Communist party in 1929, and Geldman joined a Trotskyist youth group. The interview focuses on the development of the unemployed movement after the 1934 truckers' strike and the WPA workers' strike in July 1939. Geldman describes the united participation of Trotskyists, Communists, and others in the Minneapolis labor movement in support of this strike to save the WPA from liquidation. He was convicted in 1941 for violations of the Smith Act.
Interviewer: Carl Ross

323. Green, Frank (1915–   ). 1987. 60 min. 20 p.
Green discusses growing up in the North Minneapolis Jewish community in the 1920s and 1930s. He describes the 1934 truckers' strike and Communist involvement in the Unemployed Councils. He also covers his organizing work in Rochester of hospital food workers.
Interviewer: Carl Ross

324. Hathaway, Richard (1918–   ). 1987. 90 min. 44 p.
Hathaway is the eldest son of Communist party functionary Clarence Hathaway. Although Hathaway did not spend a lot of time with his father (his parents divorced when he was young), he has some interesting insights into his father's career. He discusses his father, the Communist party, the McCarthy era, union racism, and postrevolutionary Russia.
Interviewer: Sandra Curtiss

25

325. Hemmingsen, Clarence (1895–). 1978? 60 min. 19 p.

Hemmingsen attended the Proletarian University in Chicago. He eventually came to Duluth and later to Grand Marais, where he became active in F-L politics in the 1930s. He discusses soapbox speaking, Scott Nearing, the Illinois pipefitters union, the F-LP, Elmer Benson, and his training in Chicago.
Interviewer: Tom O'Connell

326. Herness, Irwin (1901–). 1977. 60 min. 16 p.
Herness was born in Otter Tail County but grew up in South Dakota during the peak years of NPL activity, 1912–18. He attended the University of Minnesota and later became active in F-L politics. He worked for the Co-op Division of the Department of Agriculture and helped to start rural electrical cooperatives. He discusses the F-LP, Floyd B. Olson, Elmer Benson, red-baiting, the Rural Electrification Administration, and the DFL merger.
Interviewers: Steve Trimble and Tom O'Connell

327. Johnson, Nellie Stone (1904–). 1988. 2 hrs., 35 min. 48 p.
The interview covers Johnson's early life in Pine County where her father was was active in the NPL and in the co-op movement in the 1920s and 1930s. She describes coming to Minneapolis in 1924, working at the Minneapolis Athletic Club, and helping to organize Local 665 of the Hotel and Restaurant Employees Union. She also reflects on her experiences as an African American in the Minneapolis labor movement.
Interviewers: Carl Ross, Hyman Berman, Sal Salerno, Deborah Miller, Peter Rachleff, and Rhoda Gilman

328. Jorgenson, Clara (1913–), John Jorgenson, and Peter Jorgenson. 1974. 60 min. 17 p.
The Jorgensons were Pine County farmers active in farmers' movements and the People's Lobby in the 1930s. In this interview she discusses the Farm Holiday movement, the United Farmers' League, and McCarthyism.
Interviewers: Steve Trimble and others

329. Jorgenson, Clara (1913–), John Jorgenson, and Peter Jorgenson. 1976. 2 hrs. 35 p.
In this interview, they discuss farmers' movements, the Communist party, and Peter's experiences in the Abraham Lincoln Brigade in the Spanish Civil War.
Interviewers: Steve Trimble and Tom O'Connell

330. Karson, Charles (1913–). 1988. 70 min. 25 p.
Interview focuses on the lives of the Karson brothers, Charlie, Morris (Red), and Jack, in St. Paul and their affiliation with the Communist party in the late 1920s and 1930s. Touches on Karson's role as district organizer of the Young Communist League and Red's involvement in the unemployed movement, specifically the demonstrations at the State Capitol.
Interviewer: Carl Ross

331. Kykyri, John (1898–). Undated. 90 min. 23 p.
Born to Finnish immigrants in Chippewa County, Kykyri became a political journalist and member of the Communist party. In this interview he discusses Minnesota mining, the 1934 truck drivers' strike, the Communist party, Hubert Humphrey, and the CIO.
Interviewers: Steve Trimble and Tom O'Connell

332. Latz, Robert (1930–). 1988. 65 min. 20 p.
Latz discusses the life and career of his father, Reuben Latz, who was an active member of the Minneapolis Jewish community and a leader of the Cleaners, Drivers, and Laundry Workers Union, Local 183, in Minneapolis. Latz describes his father's early life in North Dakota and his later activities in the Minneapolis Workmen's Circle and as a leader of the Central Labor Union.
Interviewers: Carl Ross and Linda Schloff

333. Lebedoff, Martin (1911–). 1988. 90 min. 33 p.
Lebedoff describes the activities of the Minneapolis Jewish community in the 1920s and 1930s. He addresses the socialist activities of Jewish immigrants and the social and political differences within the community of Jewish garment workers and Jewish employers. He discusses the political struggle between the radical left-wing supporters of *Freiheit* (a radical Yiddish paper published in New York) and the more conservative members of the Workmen's Circle for control of the Labor Lyceum. Lebedoff also touches on his "old" life as an entrepreneur in the movie industry, and his continuing interest in the Jewish community.
Interviewers: Carl Ross and Linda Schloff

334. Levine, Yank. 1978. 2 hrs. 30 p.
Levine grew up in the Jewish community of Duluth with his sister, Irene Paull. He became active in the

radical communities of Duluth and New York in the 1930s. In this interview he discusses the Finnish radicalism in northern Minnesota, Irene and Henry Paull, New York theater projects, and the progressive theater community.
Interviewer: Steve Trimble

335. McMillen, Patrick J. (1895–). 1988. 60 min. 19 p.
McMillen relates several anecdotes about his life as a merchant seaman and his lifetime membership in the IWW. He describes his father's employment with the Great Northern Railway and labor-management relations.
Interviewers: Carl Ross, Richard Blin, and Virginia Hyvärinen

336. Maloney, Jack (1911–), and Don Seaverson. 1988. 9 hrs. 127 p.
Maloney participated in the labor movement of the 1930s and became active in the Motor Transport and Allied Workers Industrial Union, Local 544. He discusses IWW members and working conditions for unskilled laborers in the 1920s. He gives detailed accounts of the 1934 Minneapolis truck drivers' strike and other strikes Local 574/544 was involved in and recalls many personal memories of Carl Skoglund, the Dunne brothers, and Floyd B. Olson. Maloney's step-brother, Don Seaverson, comments throughout.
Interviewers: Sal Salerno and Peter Rachleff

337. Mayville, Jennifer (Jenny). 1977. 1 hr., 40 min. 25 p.
Mayville was active in the labor movement in Minneapolis and, briefly, in the Communist party. She married labor organizer Harry Mayville and helped him organize throughout the Midwest. She discusses the Flour City Ornamental Iron Works strike of 1935, women's auxiliary work for strikes, the F-LP, social activities in the activist community, the Communist party, and her husband's career.
Interviewer: Steve Trimble

338. Niemela, Eino (1909?–). Undated. 80 min. 27 p.
Niemela and his parents immigrated to Michigan from Finland in 1913 and in 1933 moved to Gilbert where Niemela became involved in the cooperative movement. He discusses immigration, cooperatives, the F-LP and clubs, the Unemployed Councils, business and social life in the 1930s, and the Communist party.
Interviewers: Steve Trimble and Tom O'Connell

339. Olson, Orville E. (1908–). 1982. 90 min. 27 p.
Olson describes his work as an administrator for state relief programs in rural Minnesota during the 1930s Depression, his activities in the left wing of the F-LP and as an adviser to Governor Elmer Benson, his involvement in the F-L merger with the Democratic party, and his organization of the Independent Voter's League of Minnesota. Olson was the principal organizer for Henry Wallace's 1948 presidential campaign in Minnesota. He also discusses the political activities and tactics of the left wing.
Interviewer: Carl Ross

340. Olson, Orville E. (1908–). 1977. 2 hrs. 27 p.
Olson was active in F-L politics (see above). In this interview he discusses Elmer Benson's political machine, F-L politics and labor, community and business groups, and the Democratic and F-L merger.
Interviewers: Steve Trimble and Tom O'Connell

341. Parish, Richard J. (1914–). 1989. 60 min. 11 p.
Parish, a lawyer and politician who lived in Duluth and St. Paul, held a number of elected and appointed offices, including serving in the state legislature, 1959–61, 1963–65, 1971–73. In this interview, he discusses his years as a supervisor in the WPA Workers Education Project in Duluth, tension between the AFL and CIO, political organization on the Iron Range, and his career in the state legislature.
Interviewer: Douglas Alan Bruce

342. Paszak, Joseph (1908–). 1988. 2 hrs. 44 p.
Paszak worked for Atlas Cement Co. (a division of U.S. Steel) in Duluth and was active in the United Steel Workers of America. He chaired the CIO Council in Duluth, 1936–48, but was forced out of the CIO in 1948 because of his support for the Progressive party. The interview explores his early life as the son of Polish immigrants in Wisconsin and Minnesota; conditions for working people; his activities as a union organizer; election campaigns; the racial, ethnic, and religious minorities in the Duluth labor movement; and the FBI harassment he experienced for his radical views.
Interviewers: Virginia Hyvärinen and Susanna Frenkel

Radical activists Carl Ross, right, Communist party official, and Vincent R. Dunne, leader of the Socialist Workers party and veteran of the 1934 Minneapolis truck drivers' strike, met at the Twin Cities Labor Forum in 1957.

343. Pearson, Glenn E. (1914–). 1988. 60 min. 26 p.
Pearson was born in Duluth to left-wing labor leaders Ernest and Maney Pearson. He participated in the radical youth and peace movements in Duluth in the 1940s. He organized workers at the Coolerator Co. in Duluth. As an officer in Local 1096 of the United Steel Workers of America, he helped organize other Duluth unions, notably other steelworkers, Diamond Caulk and Horseshoe Co., and newspaper unions. He spoke for the left wing of the CIO and was married to Leata Wigg.
Interviewers: Virginia Hyvärinen and Susanna Frenkel

344. Pearson, Leata Wigg. 1988. 90 min. 35 p.
Pearson was raised in Duluth. Prior to graduating from the University of Minnesota in 1939, she became active in the Young Communist League and the American Student Union. She returned to Duluth in 1939, became involved in the American Youth Congress, and married Glenn Pearson in 1941. This interview covers questioning by the FBI in the 1940s and 1950s, organizing among steelworkers, the Duluth chapter of the American Youth Congress, the University of Minnesota in the 1930s, the Young Communist League, and support for the Loyalists in the Spanish Civil War.
Interviewers: Virginia Hyvärinen and Susanna Frenkel

345. Ponikvar, Veda. 1988. 30 min. 10 p.
Ponikvar was the editor of the *Chisholm Free Press*. This interview summarizes her thoughts about the Iron Range and her belief in the value of education for miners seeking to better their social and economic condition. She talks about her own aspirations in education and her activities as a Slovene editor, publisher, and spokesperson for the Slavic community on the range.
Interviewer: Carl Ross

346. Puglisi, Frank (1907?–). Undated. 45 min. 23 p.
Puglisi's family came to Duluth from Europe in 1921. Puglisi became active in F-L politics in northern Minnesota during the 1930s. He discusses F-L clubs, patronage, Elmer Benson, and Duluth politics.
Interviewer: Tom O'Connell

347. Rolvaag, Karl F. (1913–90). 1989. 90 min. 21 p.
Rolvaag was Minnesota governor (DFL), 1963–67. This interview covers Rolvaag's childhood as son of writer, Ole Rølvaag, and his father's influence on his beliefs. Rolvaag describes his years as a lumber worker and miner in the Pacific Northwest, his membership in the IWW, and his decision to become active in DFL politics. He touches briefly on African Americans' unrest and dissatisfaction in North Minneapolis in the later years of his administration.
Interviewer: Carl Ross

348. Ross, Carl (1913–   ). 1986–88. 25 hrs., 30 min. 378 p.

Ross held a number of important positions in the Communist party and affiliated organizations, including the Young Communist League, the American Youth Congress (local, state, and national levels), and American Youth for Democracy. In the late 1940s, he headed the Minnesota-Dakotas district of the party and played a role in the CIO and the DFL. He spent two years in prison in the 1950s for sheltering a comrade who had been indicted under the Smith Act. In this series of 15 interviews, Ross discusses these events and his later career as a businessman and scholar, with an emphasis on his Finnish heritage and Finnish-American culture.
Interviewer: Hyman Berman

349. Sharp, Clarence (1891–1989). 1987. 2 hrs, 30 min. 31 p.

Interview deals with Sharp's membership in the Socialist party and the NPL, which he joined around the time of World War I, and his activities as an itinerant radical agitator in South Dakota during the early 1930s. His interview suggests that the anti-Socialist climate during and after the war led many Socialist party members to leave the party and join the NPL. Sharp deals only peripherally with his many years as the main representative of the Communist party in rural Minnesota.
Interviewer: Carl Ross

350. Sharp, Clarence (1891–1989). 1977. 60 min. 14 p.
Sharp was a Communist party organizer in rural Minnesota (see above). He had earlier been in the Socialist party and an organizer for A. C. Townley's National Producers Alliance. He discusses farmer activism, Communist party politics, and the demise of the Communist party.
Interviewers: Steve Trimble and Tom O'Connell

351. Siegler, Ruth. 1977. 60 min. 18 p.
Siegler was active in the Duluth F-LP in the 1920s and 1930s. Her husband was involved in the labor movement. She discusses F-L politics and the co-op movement.
Interviewers: Steve Trimble and Tom O'Connell

352. Skoglund, Carl (1884–1960). Undated. 2 hrs. 27 p.

Skoglund began his career in the left wing of the Socialist party. He helped form the Communist party in the United States in 1919. He was the district industrial director for the Communist party in Minnesota until he was expelled in 1928 for his Trotskyist beliefs. As a Trotskyist, he organized the Minneapolis truck drivers' strike in 1934 and was elected president of Teamsters Local 544 in 1938. He helped found the Socialist Workers party in 1938 and was convicted under the Smith Act in 1941. This interview reflects little of these activities, however, but focuses on his childhood in Sweden, with some discussion of Minnesota labor activism.
Interviewer: unknown

353. Swan, Joseph (1914–   ), and Bernice (Bunny) Fossum. 1988. 90 min. 31 p.

Swan joined the Communist party in Minneapolis in 1937. He worked for the WPA's Federal Art Project and was a member of the Artists' Union. He and Bunny Fossum reminisce about their lives as artists in the 1930s and 1940s and their activities in the Communist party. Swan also discusses how he used his art to support labor unions in their struggles.
Interviewer: Sal Salerno

354. Thomblison, James C. (1892–   ). 1972. 60 min. 32 p.

Thomblison was an IWW member in Canada. He moved to Minneapolis in the early 1920s and became involved with the labor movement. He discusses his work at Twin City Rapid Transit Co., company unions, the Amalgamated Association of Street Electric Railway and Motor Coach Employees of America, Local 1005, and several strikes.
Interviewer: Douglas Alan Bruce

355. Turner, Leo. 1988. 90 min. 17 p.
Turner grew up on the Iron Range and joined the Young Communist League at age 17. He moved to the Twin Cities in the early 1930s where he worked with the Unemployed Councils and the labor movement. Turner discusses his activities with the Unemployed Councils—particularly his arrest at a demonstration for the unemployed in Minneapolis—and his involvement in several labor struggles. He reflects on the Minnesota Finnish community and recalls his mother's involvement in the Finnish-language political theater.
Interviewer: Sal Salerno

356. Watson, Elizabeth. 1977? 45 min. 15 p.
Watson is the widow of activist Chester Watson. She discusses her work in the WPA arts projects, the Workers' Alliance, and her husband's career. Interviewers: Steve Trimble and Tom O'Connell

357. Weiss, Bertha (1907–). 1988. 1 hr., 40 min. 32 p.
Weiss recalls her childhood in Poland before World War I. Her family brought their radical beliefs with them when they emigrated to Minnesota. Weiss participated in the organization of the first branch of the Young Communist League in Minneapolis and was active in the Jewish and African-American communities as a member of the Communist party. She discusses the Communist party, the International Labor Defense, and the Scottsboro Boys. In later years she and her husband, an African American from North Minneapolis, opened a resort in the Crosby area for African Americans. She describes the relationship between the community and this resort.
Interviewer: Carl Ross

HOTEL AND RESTAURANT EMPLOYEES UNION, LOCAL 665

The Hotel and Restaurant Employees Union, Local 665, was a racially integrated AFL local founded in 1935 by a group of young, militant activists. Both the AFL and the CIO saw Local 665's participation in the Miller's Cafeteria strike of 1941 in Minneapolis as a revitalizing force in the labor movement. These interviews were conducted by Carl Ross in 1981–82.

358. Allen, Albert V. (1913–). 1981. 90 min. 25 p.
Allen was a founding member and vice-president of Local 665. He describes growing up African American in North Minneapolis in the early 1930s, his experiences as an employee at the Minneapolis Athletic Club, and his work as Minneapolis president of the NAACP, 1946–49. He also touches on his later work as organizer and president of the Clerical Workers' Union, Local 3015, at the Minneapolis airport.

359. Belmont, Rosalind Matusow (1917–). 1982. 2 hrs., 15 min. 39 p.
Belmont organized hotel maids for Local 665 in the late 1930s. She recalls her mother's activities as a member of the Hat, Cap, and Millinery Workers Union in New York and her own experience as a nursing student at the University of Minnesota, where she became active in the National Student League and the Young Communist League.

360. Brawthen, Elwin T. (Al) (1913–), and Marjorie (Margie) Brawthen (1921–). 1982. 90 min. 29 p.
Al worked in various Minneapolis hotels and was an active member of Local 665 in the 1930s. Margie organized the workers at Miller's Cafeteria, Minneapolis, and was involved in the 1941 strike.

361. Cassius, Anthony B. (1907–83). 1981, 1982. 3 hrs., 15 min. 56 p.
Cassius organized an all-African American local of waiters at the Curtis Hotel in Minneapolis in the late 1930s, which he led into Local 665. He recalls his arrival in St. Paul in 1920, his football career at St. Paul Mechanic Arts High School, and his employment at various St. Paul hotels. He also discusses the civil-rights movement in Minneapolis.

362. Fagerhaugh, Ole. 1982. 45 min. 15 p.
Fagerhaugh was an organizer for Local 665 and a member of the Communist party. He was a key player in the Miller's Cafeteria strike in Minneapolis in 1941. Fagerhaugh was a founder of and performer with the Minneapolis Theatre Union. He also discusses the influence of the Communist party on the labor movement in Minneapolis.

363. Hanson, Douglas, Victoria (Vicki) Lindesmith Hanson (1919–82), and Ole Fagerhaugh. 1981. 2 hrs., 40 min. 68 p.
Doug Hanson was a shop steward for Local 665 in the 1930s. Vicki Hanson was an active member of Local 665, particularly during the 1941 Miller's Cafeteria strike in Minneapolis. Both discuss the strike.

364. Johnson, Nellie Stone (1904–). 1981. 1 hr., 35 min. 29 p.
Johnson was born in Pine County, where her father farmed. She came to Minneapolis in 1924 and began work at the Minneapolis Athletic Club. She discusses the founding of Local 665, which she helped to organize, the truck drivers' and Miller's Cafeteria strikes, and African-American experiences in the Minneapolis labor movement.

Miners and their families paraded with signs and American flags during the 1916 Mesabi Iron Range strike.

365. Naumoff, George (1896–1987). 1981. 2 hrs., 30 min. 35 p.

Naumoff emigrated from Macedonia in 1910 and worked on the railroad in the St. Louis area. After his move to Minneapolis in 1920, he joined the Communist party. He discusses his employment at the Minneapolis Athletic Club, where he became a leading organizer and founder of Local 665. Naumoff was president of the local, 1935–74.

366. Wright, Raymond R. (1906–). 1981, 1982. 5 hrs., 50 min. 89 p.

Wright, a Finnish activist, worked as a miner, lumberman, and on the railroads in Michigan before moving to Wisconsin in the 1930s to organize farmers' protest movements. He came to Minneapolis in 1936, where he became an organizer and business agent for Local 665, a position he retained until 1971. He discusses Communist influence on Local 665, the Miller's Cafeteria strike, the Minneapolis hotel strike in 1953, and improvements in working conditions and settling of grievances.

RADICAL POLITICS
ON THE IRON RANGES

These interviews were conducted by Irene Paull in 1968 and focus on Finnish political activism, the Commu-

nist and Socialist Workers parties on the range, and the labor movement.

367. Anderson, Jacob (Jack) (1902–). 1968. 80 min. 43 p.

Born in Aitkin County of Finnish parents, Anderson as a young man worked in lumber camps, joined the IWW, and in the 1920s became involved in the co-op movement. He discusses his involvement in the Communist party and the labor movement, particularly during the 1930s Depression, and speaks of Gus Hall, Communist party leader.

368. Antilla, Anton (1888–). 1968. 1 hr., 45 min. 24 p. Restricted.

Born in Finland, Antilla immigrated to Minnesota in 1906 and worked in the mines until 1913 when he began farming. He recalls family life, the Finnish community in northern Minnesota, and his activities in radical political movements, including joining the Communist party, organizing unions, and supporting cooperative strikes.

369. Davis, Ellen Rautio. 1968. 75 min. Restricted.

Born in Cloquet of Finnish parents, Davis recalls family life and growing up in a Finnish-American community. She discusses her activity in the Communist party with her husband, Samuel K. Davis, who was the Communist party candidate for governor in 1934 and a correspondent for the Communist *Daily Worker*. She expresses her views on the struggles of African Americans and workers.

370. Foley, Alma (1909–). 1968. 90 min. Open for research only.

The secretary of the International Labor Defense in Minnesota and the Minnesota branch of the American Committee for Protection of the Foreign Born during the 1950s discusses these organizations.

371. Greenberg, Morris. 1968. 60 min. Restricted.
Greenberg started his law practice in 1922 in Eveleth and with attorney Henry Paull worked on labor cases connected with the development of the CIO and miners' unions in northern Minnesota. He discusses his legal career, his involvement with the labor movement, and Congressman John T. Bernard.

372. Harju, Walter (1900–). 1968. 60 min. 22 p. Open for research only.

Harju, born on a South Dakota homestead, discusses his organizing activities in the cooperative movement in northern Minnesota, his involvement in the Communist party and candidacy for the U.S. Congress, the Federal Writers' Project and strike, and his part in Finnish radical activities on the range.

373. Helenius, Aune (1915–). 1968. 25 min. Open for research only.

Born in Virginia, St. Louis County, of Finnish parents, Helenius discusses the Finnish cultural movement in northern Minnesota, her attendance at an IWW school in Duluth, her family's involvement in the IWW, and the life of miners and their families.

374. Johnson, Andy (1901–), and Hannah Johnson. 1968. 5 hrs. 97 p. Restricted.

Andy Johnson was born in Finland and became a miner and farmer in northern Minnesota. Hannah Johnson was the daughter of a Slovene miner from northern Minnesota. They describe the pioneer life of their parents, the efforts of radicals to effect change, and Finnish culture in northern Minnesota.

375. Koivunen, Ilmar (1916–), and Edith Koivunen. 1968. 4 hrs. 107 p. Restricted.

Koivunen, born in Mountain Iron, the son of a miner and farmer, organizer and president of the Timber Workers Union (later International Wood-

workers of America), Local 29, Duluth, and an officer in the Minnesota CIO, discusses labor struggles and union organization. Edith Koivunen describes Finnish cultural life in northern Minnesota.

376. Koski, Aily (1909–). 1968. 60 min. 22 p. Open for research only.

The daughter of a miner and farmer describes the community of Iron, St. Louis County, the life of miners, miners' organizations and unions, the farms of blacklisted miners, agriculture cooperatives, and Finnish culture in northern Minnesota.

377. Koski, Ero (1905–). 1968. 60 min. Open for research only.

Koski's father was a miner and a member of the IWW. Koski, born in Virginia, St. Louis County, discusses the Finnish cultural movement and the miners' efforts to organize labor unions.

378. Kuusisto, Martin. 1968. 75 min. 26 p. Restricted.
The secretary-treasurer of the Timber Workers Union (later International Woodworkers of America), Local 29, Duluth, 1947–58, discusses labor organizations, concentrating on the history of that union.

379. Maki, Toini. 1968. 30 min. 11 p. Open for research only.

Maki's husband, Martin Maki, was an organizer of the CIO Steel Workers Union and chairman of the Communist party in Minnesota. She recalls personal history and describes Finnish cultural life in northern Minnesota.

380. Tuominen, Urho, and Irma Tuominen. 1968. 60 min. Open for research only.

Irma Tuominen discusses her activities in left-wing Finnish politics in Minnesota in the 1930s. Urho Tuominen describes the Finnish cultural movement in Brimson, St. Louis County, where he grew up.

381. Watson, Chester (1900–), and Betty Ferguson Watson. 1968. 70 min. Open for research only.

Chester Watson, a social worker, was born in Aitkin, the son of a miner. He recalls personal history and discusses the 1930s Depression, organization of the unemployed, his presidency of the state Workers Alliance, 1936–40, and his involvement in the F-LP. The Watsons speak briefly about the Federal Art Project.

LABOR UNION MOVEMENT

Several projects on labor activists are included below. Professor Martin Duffy of the University of Minnesota Industrial Relations Center conducted a series of interviews with union leaders in 1976–77. In 1974, James Dooley interviewed union members for the Minnesota Historical Society. Professor Donald Sofchalk donated to the society the interviews he conducted for his research on Iron Range steelworkers. In several cases the same person was interviewed as part of more than one project, as indicated.

382. Bester, Earl T. (1900–   ). 1968, 1974, 1977. 5 hrs. The 1968 and 1974 interviews are restricted; the 1977 interview is open.

The son of a Michigan copper miner recalls his childhood and discusses early labor organizations on Minnesota's iron ranges and on the national level. Bester, the first president of the Steel Workers Union, Local 1028, and district director of the United Steel Workers of America Union in 1952, talks about Communist party activity within the union, the 1946 Duluth harborworkers' strike, and Governor Elmer A. Benson.

Interviewers: Helen White (1968), James Dooley (1974), and Martin Duffy (1974, 1977)

383. Bjork, Einar (1902–   ). 1977. 45 min.

Bjork was born in Sweden and immigrated to the U.S. in 1920. He recalls personal history and discusses his employment with the United States Steel Corp., 1922–68; his union activity, including serving as president of Steel Workers Union, Local 1028, Duluth; and Socialist and Communist party influences in the unions in the 1930s and 1940s.

Interviewer: Martin Duffy

384. Eberl, A. P. (Slim) (1901–   ). 1974. 60 min. 28 p.

Born in New Ulm, Eberl began working for the Chicago and Northwestern Railroad in the carshops in 1918 and was vice-president of the Tracy local union of car men in 1919. He discusses his involvement in the Teamsters Union, Local 221, 1928–41, and attempts by the Socialist Workers party to gain control of teamster unions in Minneapolis. He also was a vice-president of the Minnesota AFL in 1956 and talks about the merger of the AFL and CIO.

Interviewer: James Dooley

385. Ellis, A. Frank (1888–1976). 1973, 1974, 1975. 18 hrs., 30 min. 57 p. Open for research only.

Ellis, who began working in a meat-packing plant at the age of eight, discusses conditions in that industry, the IWW, and the Independent Union of All Workers (IUAW) in midwestern cities in the 1930s. Ellis helped organize the United Packinghouse Workers for the CIO and served that union as president of Local 9. He talks about organizing strikes, including the 1933 strike of the Geo. A. Hormel & Co. plant in Austin.

Interviewer: Martin Duffy

386. Genis, Sander D. (1895–   ). 1974, 1977. 4 hrs. 72 p.

Genis, an immigrant from Russia in 1912, started organizing clothing locals in Minneapolis and St. Paul about 1917 and conducted successful strikes. He discusses trade unionism, particularly his work as vice-president of the Amalgamated Clothing Workers of America International, 1946–75, and as president of the Minnesota CIO, 1942–45. He talks about organizing for the International Ladies Garment Workers Union in the Twin Cities, the Minneapolis Citizens Alliance, Communist party influence on the labor movement in the 1930s and 1940s, Governor Floyd B. Olson, labor support for Hubert H. Humphrey as mayoral candidate in Minneapolis in 1945, and the formation of the DFL party in 1944.

Interviewers: James Dooley (1974) and Martin Duffy (1977)

387. Harris, Myrtle. 1974. 60 min. Open for research only.

A member of the United Garment Workers Union since 1920 and a vice-president from the fifth district of the Minnesota AFL-CIO discusses her organizing activities, the 1934 truckers' strike in Minneapolis, and other union issues.

Interviewer: James Dooley

388. Johnson, Nellie Stone (1905–   ). 1975. 55 min. 20 p.

An active early member of the Hotel and Restaurant Employees Union, Local 665, a member of the F-LP, and the first African-American and woman vice-president of the Minneapolis Culinary Council discusses her background, including her family's farm, union activity in the Twin Cities, and African Americans in the union movement. This interview

was conducted for the Minnesota Black History Project.
Interviewer: David Taylor

389. Peterson, Glenn E. (1906–). 1977. 90 min.
The president, vice-president, and chairman of the grievance committee of the Steel Workers Union, Local 1028, discusses his union activities, Communists and steelworkers, labor organizer Henry Berkheimer, and the inclusion of iron-ore miners in the Steel Workers Union.
Interviewer: Martin Duffy

390. Schultz, Frank W. (1917–). 1977. 12 hrs. 144 p.
Schultz, who worked at the Geo. A. Hormel & Co. plant in Austin, 1931–73, and was president of the Packinghouse Workers Union, Local 9, 1945–70, discusses the Independent Union of All Workers in Austin, the 1933 strike at the Hormel plant, Communists and unions, the McCarthy era, and the strike at the Wilson Co. in 1959 in Albert Lea. He also comments on A. Frank Ellis, Jay Hormel, and other people involved in union activities in Austin.
Interviewer: Martin Duffy

391. Swanson, Sam E. (?–1972). 1968, 1969. 3 hrs., 30 min.
A labor organizer for the Steel Workers Union in northern Minnesota during the 1930s and 1940s and secretary of the Iron Range Industrial Union Council discusses unemployment and the CIO in the 1930s, newspapers' opinions of union organization efforts, independent mines, and the benefits of unions.
Interviewers: Helen White (1968) and Donald Sofchalk (1968, 1969)

392. Tomasich, Andrew. 1971. 75 min. Open for research only.
Tomasich worked in the coal mines in the eastern U.S. before moving to northern Minnesota. He discusses mining, labor grievances, his activities as a CIO organizer during the 1930s, the split between the AFL and CIO, and the Communist party and unionism.
Interviewer: Donald Sofchalk

393. Wright, Raymond R. (1906–). 1977. 3 hrs.
Wright describes his early life working in logging camps, paper mills, sawmills, and copper mines, on

farms, and in various cities of the Midwest and discusses his work as a labor organizer and union administrator for the Hotel and Restaurant Employees Union, Local 665, Minneapolis, 1936–71.
Interviewer: Martin Duffy

FARM HOLIDAY ASSOCIATION

The Farm Holiday Association was a farmers' movement that fought to increase farm prices and secure relief from mortgage foreclosures in the 1930s. Professors H. Warren Gardner, David L. Nass, and Maynard Brass of Southwest State University in Marshall conducted the interviews, 1972–75, in a Minnesota Historical Society project. Most of the interviews are located at the Southwest Minnesota Historical Center in Marshall (Southwest); others are at the West Central Minnesota Historical Center, University of Minnesota–Morris (Rwest central).

394. Bosch, John. 1972. 50 min. 36 p. (Southwest)
A retired Kandiyohi County insurance executive and former president of the Minnesota Farm Holiday Assn. discusses the economic and social conditions that gave rise to the Farm Holiday movement and his work with it.

395. Dahlquist, Oscar. 1973. 45 min. 23 p. (Southwest)
A farmer from the Slayton area discusses the Rural Electrification Administration.

396. Ebeling, Louis. 1973. 50 min. 33 p. (Southwest)
Rushmore farmer discusses the Rural Electrification Administration.

397. Farm Holiday Association. 1973. 30 min. 7 p. (Southwest)
Selected excerpts from the Southwest Minnesota Historical Center's collection of interviews on the Farm Holiday Assn.

398. Hanson, N. P. 1976. 45 min. (Rwest central)
A county agent from Pope County discusses the Farm Holiday Assn. and his work during the 1930s.

399. Haroldson, Clint. 1974. 90 min. 30 p. (Southwest)
A Renville County farmer and Farm Holiday Assn. organizer in central and northern Minnesota discusses the association's activities and life during the 1930s Depression.

A Farm Holiday mortgage strike led these men to protest against a foreclosure sale at the Lac qui Parle County courthouse in Madison one cold January day in 1933.

400. Hassenstab, Arthur F. 1972. 45 min. 36 p. (Southwest)

A banker from Wabasso discusses the effects of the 1930s Depression on the banking industry.

401. Johnson, Ernest. 1972. 50 min. 24 p. (Southwest)

A farmer in Jackson and Watonwan counties recalls the Farm Holiday Assn. march on the State Capitol in 1933.

402. Johnson, William. 1972. 50 min. 34 p. (Southwest)

Owner and editor of the *Ivanhoe Times,* Lincoln County. Accompanied by three photos and 30 slides of the interview.

403. Lange, Walter R. 1975. 61 min. (Southwest)

The retired president of the Pipestone National Bank discusses banking during the 1930s Depression and the Farm Holiday Assn. in Pipestone County, farm prices, farm mortgage foreclosures, and the New Deal.

404. Lund, Clarence. 1973. 50 min. 26 p. (Southwest)

A farmer near Lake Lillian, Kandiyohi County, recalls the Farm Holiday Assn. march on the State Capitol in 1933.

405. Lund, Guy H. 1975. 60 min. (Southwest)

A seed-corn salesman recalls his work for the Farmers Union in southwest Minnesota and activities of the Farm Holiday Assn. in Lincoln County.

406. Meehl, Percy. 1973. 90 min. 45 p. (Southwest)

A Lyon County judge and former county attorney discusses his work, the 1930s Depression in southwest Minnesota, and the 1934 Farm Holiday Assn. march on the Swift Packing Co. meat-packing plant in Marshall.

407. Nystrom, William. 1972. 75 min. (Southwest)

A farmer and state legislator, 1935–37, from Worthington discusses the Farmers Union and its interests in the Farm Holiday Assn., New Deal legislation, and the Rural Electrification Administration.

408. Olson, David E. 1973. 50 min. 29 p. (Southwest)

A Jackson County farmer comments on New Deal legislation.

409. Peterson, Roy. 1973. 60 min. 23 p. (Southwest)

A dairy-products distributor from Benson discusses the F-LP, the 1935 convention of the Minnesota Farm Holiday Assn., Governor Elmer A. Benson, and the activities of the NPL and the National Farmers Organization.

410. Peterson, Roy. 1973. 2 hrs. 22 p. (Southwest) and (Rwest central)

A Benson man (see above) comments on his involvement in the NPL, Farm Holiday Assn., and other 1930s political organizations.

411. Sanders, Parker. 1973. 50 min. 18 p. (Southwest)

A Redwood Falls farmer comments on New Deal farm legislation and the Rural Electrification Administration.

412. Tatge, Orville. 1973. 2 hrs., 30 min. 30 p. (Southwest) and (Rwest central)

The former president of the Swift County National Farmers Organization discusses its activities, agricultural conditions during the 1930s Depression, and political activity in west-central Minnesota.

413. Tkach, Andrew. 1972. 45 min. 23 p. (Southwest)

A Jackson County farmer reminisces about the NPL and Farm Holiday Assn. activity.

414. Topel, Charles. 1972. 45 min. 23 p. (Southwest)

A Lyon County farmer remembers the 1930s Depression and the beginnings of the Rural Electrification Administration.

415. Torstenson, Oscar. 1973. 50 min. 36 p. (Southwest)

A Lac qui Parle farmer and director of the Minnesota Valley Electric Light and Power Cooperative comments on the Rural Electrification Administration.

WOMEN'S INTERNATIONAL LEAGUE FOR PEACE AND FREEDOM IN MINNESOTA

The Women's International League for Peace and Freedom (WIL) was founded to protest World War I. Its primary objectives were total and universal disarmament, abolition of violence and encouragement of peaceful settlements of conflicts, and the development of a world organization to promote political, social, and economic cooperation among nations. In 1972, Gloria Thompson, a Moorhead State College student, conducted a series of interviews with members of the WIL for the Minnesota Historical Society.

416. Hawkins, Madge (1882–1980). 1972. 60 min.

Hawkins, a schoolteacher, was involved in the NPL of North Dakota, the F-LP in Minnesota, and the WIL, which she joined in the 1930s. She married Oscar Hawkins.

417. Hendrickson, Viena Johnson (1898–1980). 1972. 60 min.

Hendrickson immigrated to Minnesota from Finland as an infant with her parents. She was active in the F-LP in the 1930s and 1940s, served as a representative of the International Ladies Garment Workers Union, 1952–53, and was an active member and president of the WIL, 1935–71.

418. Meili, Olive (1895–   ). 1972. 60 min.

Meili joined the WIL in the 1930s and has served as an officer.

419. Sibley, Marjorie. 1972. 30 min. Restricted.

A college librarian, Sibley moved to Minnesota in 1948, became active in the WIL, and was state president of the organization during the Joseph McCarthy period.

BUSINESS AND LABOR IN DULUTH

In 1980–81, Barbara J. Sommer of the Northeast Minnesota Historical Center conducted a series of interviews to document the history of Duluth area businesses and their relationship to labor unions. These interviews are located at the Northeast Minnesota Historical Center at Duluth.

420. Bridges, Russell, and Helen Wingrove Bridges. 1981. 60 min. (Duluth)

Two union activists discuss the organization of the Retail Clerks Union, Local 1116, Duluth; the 1937 and 1946–47 strikes against the Glass Block Department Store; and the International Head of the Lakes Council.

421. McMillen, Patrick. 1980. 92 min. (Duluth)

A retired ship's cook describes his work for the IWW, the organization's objectives, his attempts to recruit members, the role of women in the IWW, changes in IWW ideology, and his work as a cook for various shipping lines.

422. Miller, Curtis. 1981. 75 min. (Duluth)

The former editor of *Labor World*, 1951–65, and president of the Lake Superior Newspaper Guild discusses the Duluth Industrial Union Council, the National Right to Work Committee, and the relationship of *Labor World* to the major Duluth daily newspapers.

423. Slaughter, Edward L. 1980. 2 hrs. (Duluth)
A union employee describes his work with the International Longshoremen's Assn., the impact of World War I on union activities, organizing the waterfront in Duluth during the 1930s, and union attitudes toward the IWW and the Communist party.

INDIVIDUAL INTERVIEWS
AND REMINISCENCES

The interviews with the radical and political activists listed below were collected by the Minnesota Historical Society individually as recollections of life in Minnesota in general. Also below are miscellaneous interviews from the regional historical centers in Moorhead, Mankato, Morris, and Marshall.

424. Basford, Harry (1908–74). 1973. 75 min. 37 p. (Moorhead)
State representative, 1949–61, and founder of the Grass Roots Fund for Farmers and the Becker County Farmers Union.

425. Benson, Elmer A. (1895–1985). 1963, 1964, 1969. 4 hrs., 15 min. 160 p. The 1969 interview is restricted.
Benson discusses his political career as F-L governor, 1937–39, state commissioner of banks, 1933–35, U.S. Senator, 1935–37, and chairman of the Progressive party, 1948.
Interviewers: James Bormann, Russell Fridley, and Lucile Kane (1963); Carl Chrislock and Lucile Kane (1964); Russell Fridley, Robert Goff, Lila Johnson, and James Pederson (1969)

426. Benson, Elmer A. (1895–1985). 1973. 80 min. 17 p. (Rwest central); 1974. 60 min. 27 p. (Moorhead)
The Minnesota governor, 1937–39, and U.S. Senator, 1935–37, from Appleton discusses the F-LP, the WPA in Minnesota, and legislation during the 1930s Depression.

427. Benson, Louis. 1977. 60 min.

Governor Elmer A. Benson's brother recalls his family background and discusses the origins of the F-LP, conflicts between farmers and laborers, radical politics, and a variety of other political topics.
Interviewer: Steve Trimble

428. Bernard, John Toussaint (1893–1983). 1968?, 1969, 1977. 10 hrs. The 1968? interview is open for research only; the 1969 interview is open; the 1977 interview is restricted.
Born in Corsica, Bernard emigrated to the U.S. in 1907. He recalls personal history and describes working in the iron mines of northern Minnesota, 1911–17. He discusses activities in the F-LP, including his term as U.S. Congressman, 1937–39, and his involvement in the labor movement, particularly in organizing miners. An accomplished raconteur, he tells many stories about labor union and political figures.
Interviewers: Irene Paull (1968?, 1969) and Steve Trimble (1977)

429. Bester, Connie Poppenberg (1904–). 1969. 1 hr., 50 min. Open for research only.
She discusses family background and the career of her husband, Earl Bester, a CIO organizer on the iron ranges. Her daughter Charlene also comments.
Interviewer: Helen White

430. Bester, Earl T. (1900–). 1978. 30 min. 16 p.
Bester organized steelworkers on the Iron Range. He was district director of the United Steel Workers of America and involved in F-L and DFL politics. In this interview, which was conducted as part of the Minnesota Historical Society's Hubert H. Humphrey Oral History Project, Bester discusses how his career and activities intersected with Humphrey's career.
Interviewer: Arthur Naftalin

431. Coover, Oscar, Jr. (1920–). 1977. 3 hrs. Restricted.
Active in radical politics and union organizing, he discusses his family, particularly his father, Oscar Coover, Sr., a leader in the 1934 truckers' strike in Minneapolis.
Interviewer: Steve Trimble

432. Covey, Wes (1890–). 1977. 60 min.
Covey began working for the Burlington railroad

in 1907 and was active in labor unions. He recalls riding the rails during the 1930s Depression, railroad accidents, hobos, and Hoovervilles.
Interviewer: Martin Duffy

433. Day, Walter E. (1880–1969). 1967. 75 min. 33 p. Open for research only.

A state representative as a member of the NPL, 1919–33, and a member of the F-L and DFL parties, 1937–59, discusses family history, including homesteading near Bagley, Arthur C. Townley and the NPL, the state legislature in the 1920s and 1930s, and Governor Floyd B. Olson.
Interviewer: Russell Fridley

434. Dobbs, Farrell (1907–83), and Marvel S. Dobbs. 1977. 4 hrs. Open for research only.

The Dobbses, who grew up in Minneapolis, discuss personal history, the development of their political philosophy, Carl Skoglund, and their membership in the Communist and Socialist Workers parties. They also talk about radical unionism and describe in detail the 1934 truckers' strike in Minneapolis and their involvement in organizing it.
Interviewers: Tom O'Connell and Steve Trimble

435. DuBois, Benjamin F., Sr. (1885–1981). 1967. 2 hrs., 15 min.

A banker from Sauk Centre talks about life there in the 1880s and 1890s and about his family, particularly his father, Julian DuBois. He reminisces about political and economic affairs, including the NPL, the Communist party in the 1930s and 1940s, the Independent Bankers Assn., U.S. foreign policy, and Minnesota politics. He also comments on a number of political figures and author Sinclair Lewis.
Interviewers: Russell Fridley, Robert Goff, and Lila Johnson

436. Dunne, Vincent Raymond (1889–1970). 1969. 1 hr., 45 min. 45 p. Restricted.

A major organizer of the 1934 truckers' strike in Minneapolis describes his boyhood in Kansas and on a Minnesota farm, migrant work on the West Coast, and his experiences in the IWW and the Communist party in the 1920s. He discusses ideological differences within the Communist party and the Socialist Workers party, organizing labor groups, and the 1934 strike.
Interviewer: Lila Johnson

437. Ellis, A. Frank (1888–1976). 1974. 40 min. (OMankato)

A labor organizer and the first president of United Packinghouse Workers of America, Local 9, discusses the union's 1933 strike against the Geo. A. Hormel & Co. in Austin.

438. Geldman, Max (1905–89). 1977. 4 hrs. Restricted.
An immigrant from Poland in 1914 who settled in Minnesota in 1929 recalls family background and his childhood in New York and describes his introduction to radical politics, the Young Communist League, and his involvement in the Communist party. He discusses unions and strikes, including his activities in the 1939 WPA strike, and his subsequent arrest, conviction under the Smith Act in 1941, and imprisonment in the federal prison in Sandstone.
Interviewer: Steve Trimble

439. Harju, Walter (1900–). 1977. 4 hrs. Restricted.
Born on a South Dakota homestead, Harju discusses his family background, his work as a harvest hand, and his developing political consciousness and labor activism in northern Minnesota. He was interested in syndicalism and joined the Future Leaders and the Young Workers League. He was active in the NPL, the F-LP, the Writers' Union, and labor organizing efforts on the West Coast in the mid-1920s. He ran for lieutenant-governor of Wisconsin in the 1930s on the Communist party ticket, managed the *Farmers' National Weekly*, and worked in the cooperative movement in northern Minnesota with various farmer and labor organizations.
Interviewer: Steve Trimble

440. Hemmingsen, Clarence (1895–). 1977. 2 hrs., 30 min.
This son of Norwegian immigrant parents recalls his family background, childhood, and apprenticeship as a pipefitter. He discusses his political and labor union activities, including membership in the Socialist party and the Proletarian Party of America, attempts to organize a national F-LP, and being expelled from the Pipefitters Union in the early 1930s. Hemmingsen also talks about moving to the north shore of Lake Superior and operating a small resort.
Interviewer: James Youngdale

441. Hess, Robert E. (1918–). 1969, 1970. 1 hr., 45 min. 29 p.

The president of the Minnesota CIO, 1951–56, and executive vice-president of the Minnesota AFL-CIO, 1956–66, discusses family background, his childhood in St. Paul, early union activities including organizing the Minnesota Mining and Manufacturing Co., St. Paul, for the CIO in the late 1940s, the merger of the AFL and the CIO, the DFL party, legislation affecting organized labor, and the 1959 packinghouse-workers' strike of the Wilson Co. in Albert Lea. He talks about his responsibilities as a member of the University of Minnesota Board of Regents, 1959–66, and comments on various political figures including Orville L. Freeman and Karl F. Rolvaag.
Interviewer: Lila Johnson

442. Johnson, Francis A. 1973. 60 min. 27 p.
The son of Magnus Johnson (1871–1936) remembers his father's career in the state legislature, 1915–17 and 1919–23, and the U.S. Congress, 1923–25 and 1933–35, and as the F-L candidate for governor in 1922 and 1926. He also recalls other Farmer-Laborites and Nonpartisan Leaguers of the 1920s and 1930s.
Interviewer: Bruce Larson

443. Johnson, Walter. 1973. 20 min. 12 p. (Moorhead)
Otter Tail County farmer and Progressive party gubernatorial candidate in 1948 discusses the events surrounding the campaign.

444. Kivi, Karen. 1973. 60 min. 25 p. (Moorhead)
A librarian at Moorhead State University discusses the activities of the Finnish community in Crosby during the 1930s Depression.

445. Koski, Leo A. (1912–   ). 1977. 60 min.
The son of Finnish immigrants in northern Minnesota discusses family history, his activities as a Young Communist League organizer in Michigan and on the Mesabi Range in the 1930s, the Finnish cultural movement, and later developments in Marxist ideology.
Interviewers: Tom O'Connell and Steve Trimble

446. Larson, George O. 1973. 90 min. 68 p. (Southwest)
A retired Minneota farmer discusses life in the 1930s Depression and NPL activity in Lyon County.

447. McGrath, Thomas. 1973. 50 min. 22 p. (Moorhead)

A former member of the Communist party in the U.S. comments on its development and on the 1930s Depression as it affected the Red River valley near Moorhead.

448. Martinson, Henry R. 1973. 45 min. 27 p. (Moorhead)
Includes discussion of the Socialist party in North Dakota, the NPL, and labor unions.

449. Murphy, Lawrence W. 1974. 45 min. (OMankato)
A retired manager comments on work at the Geo. A. Hormel & Co. meat-packing plant in Austin, 1923–64, and on the 1933 strike there.

450. Nygaard, Karl E. (Nygard, Emil). 1973. 60 min. 21 p. (Moorhead)
The mayor of Crosby, elected in 1932 and the first Communist mayor in the U.S., discusses the Communist party, his mayoral campaign, the New Deal, and World War II as it affected American Communists.

451. Paull, Irene Levine (1901–81). 1977. 1 hr., 50 min. Restricted.
Born in Duluth, the daughter of Ukrainian Jews recalls her childhood and the origins of her socialist beliefs and interest in the Communist party. She discusses her role and that of her attorney husband, Henry Paull, in leftist politics and labor organizations in the 1930s and 1940s, as well as the nature and effectiveness of political literature, including her own writing. She comments on the F-LP and various political figures.
Interviewer: Steve Trimble

452. Petersen, Hjalmar (1890–1968). 1963. 60 min. 20 p. Open for research only.
Petersen discusses his political career as F-L governor, 1936–37, state representative, 1931–35, lieutenant-governor, 1935–36, and railroad and warehouse commissioner, 1937–43.
Interviewers: Russell Fridley and Lucile Kane

453. Rezatto, Helen Graham. 1973. 45 min. (Southwest)
An assistant professor of literature at Southwest State University in Marshall reflects on NPL activity in North Dakota and on William Langer as governor of North Dakota, 1933–34 and 1937–39.

454. Shields, James M. 1968. 75 min. 32 p.

An employee of the National Labor Relations Board in Minneapolis, 1936–47, recalls his family background and childhood and discusses working for the Federal Emergency Relief Administration and WPA, the F-LP in the 1930s, the merger of the F-LP and Democratic party, and Elmer A. Benson.
Interviewers: Russell Fridley and Lila Johnson

455. Vapaa, Ivor. 1968. 2 hrs., 15 min. Open for research only.

A Finnish immigrant to the U.S. in 1908 discusses his labor background, the IWW, and the *Industrialisti,* an IWW newspaper he edited in Duluth.
Interviewer: Helen White

Archival and Manuscript Collections

Included here are selected personal papers and records of organizations and businesses in the collections of the Minnesota Historical Society, the University of Minnesota Archives (Uarch), the Immigration History Research Center (IHRC), and the regional historical centers at Moorhead (Moorhead), Marshall (Southwest), and Duluth (Duluth). Also included are governors' papers and selected agency records from the Minnesota State Archives, which are housed at the Minnesota Historical Society. The collections at the MHS Research Center are accessible through the computerized catalog. The location of collections not at the society is given in each entry.

For more detailed descriptions of the MHS items listed, see "Annotated Survey of Holdings on 20th-Century Radicalism in Minnesota in the Minnesota Historical Society Division of Archives and Manuscripts" by Karen Wilson, "A Survey of Minnesota Labor Materials in the Papers of the Great Northern Railway and Northern Pacific Railroad Companies in the Minnesota Historical Society" by Karen Wilson and John Wickre, and "A Survey of the Minnesota State Archives: A Listing of Radical/Labor/Farm Movement Materials in the Minnesota Governors' Papers, 1931-1942" by Jerry Flower. All are available at the reference desk of the MHS Research Center.

456. Adams, Elmer Ellsworth (1861–1950), and Family. Papers, 1860–1951. 84 rolls microfilm.
Adams was a Republican politician and businessman who also edited the *Fergus Falls Journal*. He served several terms in the Minnesota House of Representatives and Senate. Papers include correspondence and documents on the Socialist party, the NPL, the America First Assn., the Farm Holiday Assn., and the F-LP. The collection also includes information on gubernatorial campaigns, 1920–40, particularly literature opposing Floyd B. Olson, Elmer Benson, and Ernest Lundeen.

457. Amalgamated Clothing Workers of America, Twin Cities Joint Board. Records, 1919–28, 1947. 1 box.
The ACWA was an early industrial union within the AFL. The collection contains correspondence to and from Elizabeth Gurley Flynn, Sander Genis, Forrest Edwards, and others regarding the ACWA's relationship to the Working People's NPL, William Mahoney, the Progressive Political Convention of 1924, and the IWW.

458. America First Association, St. Paul. Papers, 1917–35. 32 items.
The collection includes minutes, resolutions, and circulars from the association, which was organized to promote patriotism and crush sedition. Includes information on the alleged promotion of disloyalty by Arthur C. Townley and the NPL.

459. American Federation of Labor. Correspondence with Local Affiliates, 1933–47. 1 roll microfilm (negative). Originals located in the George Meany Memorial Archives, Washington, D.C.
Correspondence mainly concerns the Minneapolis truck drivers' strike of 1934, the Duluth Federated Trades Assembly, and the Minneapolis Central Labor Union, with references to Communist activity in the unions. (Note: Much of the microfilm is illegible.)

460. Anderson, Eugenie Moore (1909–   ). Papers, 1945–73. 19 boxes. Restricted.
Anderson was active in DFL party politics, 1940s–60s. She played a key role in ousting radical activists from the newly merged DFL and advised Hubert Humphrey to disclaim any support from Communists. Box 13 contains items relating to her political activities, 1945–58.

461. Anderson and Blegen, comps., ca. 1933–64. Minnesota Political Party Platforms, 1849–1942. 3 boxes.

Socialist Workers party candidates, left to right, Warren Creel, Dorothy Schultz, Grace Carlson, and Chester Johnson posed for a photographer while filing petitions to have their names on the ballot about 1946, when Grace Carlson ran for the United States Senate. Third-party candidates often filed petitions as an alternative to paying the filing fee to get on the ballot.

Collection was compiled by William Anderson and Theodore C. Blegen and contains texts of political party platforms and resolutions, as well as related correspondence. Files for the years 1906–18 contain platforms, resolutions, and notes about the Socialist Party of America (formerly the Public Ownership party) and the Socialist Labor party, which became the Industrial Labor party. The years 1920–42 include items about the Working People's NPL, the Progressive Republican party, the F-LP, the NPL, the Workers party, the Communist party, the Socialist Workers party, and the Independent Progressive Voters. The years 1938–43 include research notes by the compilers, notes on the project, a partial draft of a manuscript, and correspondence between the compilers and such organizations as the F-LP, the NPL, the Working People's NPL, the Democratic party, the Republican party, the Union party and miscellaneous Union parties, the Prohibition party, the Communist party, the Socialist Workers party, and the Socialist Labor party.

462. Anonymous, comp. Correspondence and Other Papers Relating to the Minnesota Legislature, 1933–39. 2 boxes.

This collection contains correspondence, resolutions, petitions, and copies of legislative bills relating to the Minnesota legislature, 1933–39. Of interest is a 1935 resolution from the Hennepin County Farmer-Labor Women's Club supporting Marion Le Sueur, Florence Cook, and Paul Amidon for appointment to the State Board of Education.

463. Anti-Compulsory Military Drill League, University of Minnesota–Twin Cities. Collection, ca. 1925. 4 items. (Uarch)

Ephemeral materials including open letter, handbills, and petitions to end compulsory drill at the University of Minnesota, 1925.

464. Aufderheide, Herman (1892–1958). Papers, 1933–49. 1 box.

Aufderheide served as secretary to Floyd B. Olson and Hjalmar Petersen, 1935–36, and participated in many local civic organizations. Papers include correspondence concerning patronage during the administrations of Olson and Benson, hostility between F-L activists and the Farm Holiday Movement, the Farmer-Labor Political Federation, and the League for Independent Political Action.

465. Ball, Joseph Hurst (1905–   ). Papers, 1940–48. 4 boxes.

Ball wrote about state politics for the *St. Paul Pioneer Press and Dispatch* and was appointed in 1940 by Governor Harold Stassen to fill the U.S. Senate seat of deceased Senator Ernest Lundeen. Ball was a Republican who supported the internationalist policies of President Roosevelt. He served in the Senate until 1949. His papers include two folders on "communist subversive activities" and some anti-Communist speeches.

466. Basford, Harry (1908–74). Papers, 1948–67. (Moorhead)

Basford served in the Minnesota House of Representatives, 1949–61. He was a founder of the Grass Roots Fund for Farmers and president of the Becker County Farmers' Union. Papers include correspondence, clippings, and papers relating to the Grass Roots Fund and the Farmers' Movement.

467. Beeman, St. Clair (1910–   ). Papers, 1943–78. 11 boxes.

Beeman was active in International Union of Electrical Workers (CIO), Local 1160, 1940s–60s. The collection includes printed materials from both the IUE and its predecessor, the United Electrical, Radio and Machine Workers, which was expelled from the CIO in 1949. Box 1 includes 3 folders dealing with alleged Communist influence in the UE and its expulsion from the CIO. Also of interest are newspaper clippings; UE and IUE newspapers from 1950–51, including some from Locals 1139, 1140, and 1145; political files regarding Joseph McCarthy; and a scrapbook of newspaper clippings from 1949 and 1950 regarding the expulsion of Communists from the CIO.

468. Benson, Elmer Austin (1895–1985). Papers, undated, 1931–63, 1973–74. 27 boxes.

Elmer Benson was appointed to the U.S. Senate in Dec. 1935 by Governor Olson. He was governor of Minnesota, 1937–39. Benson played a key role in progressive political organizations such as the Farmer-Labor Assn. and the CIO Political Action Committee. Items of interest from 1936–38 concern charges of Communist influence in the F-LP. Papers from 1950–54 include information on McCarthyism, the People's Republic of China, the USSR, world peace, the Farmers' Union, anti-Semitism, and Socialist party activity in the U.S. (Note: See also Benson's papers in the Governors' Papers, State Archives.)

469. Bernard, John Toussaint (1893–1983). Papers, undated, 1934–62, 1973. 1 box.

Bernard, an active left-wing labor leader and member of the F-LP in Eveleth, was elected to Congress in 1936. He worked with the CIO in organizing the Iron Range and, in 1943, with the United Electrical, Radio, and Machine Workers (CIO) Political Action Committee in Chicago. He was the only congressman to vote against the embargo on arms shipments to Spain in 1937. He later appeared before the House Un-American Activities Committee for his association with Communist fronts. The majority of his papers (1936–56) give information about his participation in the F-LP, his term in Congress, campaign literature, newspaper clippings, his antifascist activities, and his work with the Steel Workers Organizing Committee of the CIO.

470. Berninghausen, David Knipe. Papers, ca. 1948–72. 12 boxes. (Uarch)

Berninghausen was active in the American Library Assn. Papers include correspondence and printed materials dealing with intellectual freedom, censorship, and the loyalty oath in libraries, 1948–72.

471. Bester, Earl T. (1900–   ). Papers, 1937–67. 3 boxes.

Bester was a founding organizer of the United Steel Workers (USW) of America (CIO) in 1936. In 1952 he became director of District 33 of the USW-CIO in Duluth. His correspondence and papers include information about his struggle with Communists in the CIO, the 1948 senatorial race between DFL-er Hubert H. Humphrey and Republican incumbent Joseph Ball, and miscellaneous materials on Minnesota politics, 1941–64, including a 1949 anti-Communist broadside about the Duluth City Civil Service and a pamphlet entitled *The People vs. the Corporation* by the Minnesota CIO Council. The collection also includes materials on non-Communist affidavits for District 33 (1956–57) of the USW-CIO.

472. Borchardt, Lena L. (1892–1972). "I Lived a Full Life: Reminiscences," 1969–72. 2 folders.

These are the handwritten memoirs of Lena Louise Goldeman Borchardt, a Swiss woman who farmed with her husband, Arthur, in Willow River, Pine County. In section five she talks about radical politics in North Minneapolis and Willow River, 1900–30s. She discusses the NPL, its conflicts with the Minnesota Home Guard during World War I, F-L activities, and the family's membership in the Communist party, which they joined in 1936.

473. Brandborg, Charles W. (1847–1916), and Family. Papers, undated, 1887–1977. 3 boxes.

Brandborg was active in the Farmers Alliance, and most of his children were active in the Socialist Labor party of Minnesota. The collection includes biographical data, correspondence, clippings, and scrapbook materials, which contain information about the Farmers Alliance, the Socialist Labor party, and national political issues. Also included are speeches by Brandborg, Eugene Debs, and Daniel DeLeon.

474. Brin, Fanny Fligelman (1896–1958). Papers, 1896–1958. 25 boxes.

Brin was active in various peace organizations and interested in Jewish welfare and the participation of women in public affairs. Her papers include materials from the Women's International League for Peace and Freedom, the Socialist party, the Communist party, and various other radical organizations, as well as antiradical, anti-Communist items.

475. Broadside Collection. Undated, 1840–1941. 1 box.

Folder 13 (1901–41) contains a variety of items relating to radicalism in Minnesota, primarily fliers and announcements for meetings and publications. Items of interest include a 1912 pamphlet announcing a lecture by Nellie Zeh on Socialism, a 1918 broadside for a NPL meeting, a 1919 Socialist party broadside for the Kate Richards O'Hare farewell, a 1920 broadside advertisement for *Justice Held for Ransom* by Grant S. Youmans, and an anti-Townley book.

476. Broms, Wilbur S. (1912–). Papers, 1917–79. 1 box. Restricted.

Broms's mother, Clara Strong Broms, and father, Allen, were active in the Socialist party and later the Communist party. Broms grew up in St. Paul's community of radical activists. He joined the Young Communist League in the 1930s and later became a singer with the Metropolitan Opera. His papers contain correspondence, articles, and clippings concerning his parents' activities, the role of music and

art in the Communist party, and the federal art and music projects of the WPA in Minnesota.

477. Brown, Edward Fullerton (1891–). Papers, undated, 1915–16, 1923–62. 6 boxes.

Brown was an active anti-Communist who worked closely with Emil Holmes from the early 1930s to 1962 and was involved with the American Security Alliance Organization and the Minnesota State Union party (1936). Box 4 includes correspondence from the 1930s–40s, which expresses Holmes's opposition to Communism. The correspondence also indicates interest in a merger between the Union party and the F-LP, which died because of Communist influence in the F-LP.

478. Bruce, Douglas Alan. Papers, 1933–72. 1 box.

Bruce was Minnesota director of the WPA Worker Education Program. Includes items relating to Elmer Benson's 1938 gubernatorial campaign, the Minneapolis Central Council for the Unemployed, the WPA strike, the People's Lobby in 1937, and the assassination of teamster official Patrick J. Corcoran.

479. Bullard, Polly Caroline (1881–1949). "Remembrances of Things Past: The Reminiscences and Diary of Polly Caroline Bullard." Originals in the possession of Mrs. Ernest W. Kohlsaat, St. Paul.

The diary describes life in St. Paul in the early 1900s and later in Eveleth, where Bullard was a teacher. She notes the strong socialist element among the Finnish people.

480. Bullis, Harry Amos (1890–1963). Papers, 1898–1963. 26 boxes, 30 vols.

Bullis was president of General Mills, 1942–48, and board chairman, 1948–58. He was active in a variety of business, civic, and political organizations. Volume 21, in particular, contains correspondence, clippings, and other items about the National Association of Manufacturers (NAM), of which Bullis was a prominent member. NAM was a group of small to medium-sized industries whose leaders joined together to protect their businesses from both big business and labor. The volume includes correspondence with the Citizens Alliance of Minneapolis and recommendations that the U.S. should follow the British system of defeating radicalism by adopting such measures as social insurance and low-cost housing, thereby co-opting the radicals' platforms.

481. Burnquist, Joseph Alfred Arner (1879–1961). Papers, undated, 1884–1960. 28 boxes.

Burnquist, a Republican, served in various state and elected offices, including attorney general, lieutenant-governor, and governor, 1915–21. Boxes 4–21 of his papers contain materials by and about the Commission of Public Safety and its repression of political activity in the years around World War I. These include correspondence and reports from the commission concerning IWW activities on the Iron Range, surveillance of the NPL, and allegations of subversive activity and disloyalty among Minnesota's foreign-born population. Also included are some transcripts of the commission's meetings in 1918. (Note: See also Burnquist's papers in the Governors' Papers, State Archives.)

482. Cain, Agnes Myrtle (1884–1980). Papers, 1923–78. 1 box.

Cain served in the Minnesota House of Representatives for northeast Minneapolis, 1923–25. A prominent labor leader, she had been endorsed by the Working People's NPL. Cain also served as a board member of the National Woman's party and worked with the Women's Trade Union League of Minneapolis. She remained active in the labor movement after her election defeat in 1924.

483. Carpenters and Joiners Brotherhood of America, Local 87, St. Paul. Papers, undated, 1885–1960. 1 box.

The collection includes minutes of meetings, journals, forms, and circulars concerning boycotts, strikes, and alternative tactics and debates over the question of labor's participation in politics.

484. Central Labor Union of Minneapolis and Hennepin County. Papers, 1912–62. 61 boxes.

This collection documents the activities of the Central Labor Union and its predecessor, the Minneapolis Trades and Labor Assembly. It contains substantial materials about the AFL, Communist activities within the AFL, Communist activities within the building trades, the Citizens Alliance, local branches of the Communist party, conflicts between the Socialist Workers party and the Communist party, May Day rallies, the Minneapolis truck drivers' strike of 1934, the Worker's Party of America, the League of Struggle for Negro Rights, the Public Ownership League, the Labor party, the Farmers' NPL, the Working People's NPL, the F-LP, the DFL, and the

Independent Labor party. Also included are records and correspondence regarding the Minneapolis Labor School, Sacco and Vanzetti, the House Un-American Activities Committee, the Ole J. Arness case (1917) of a Minneapolis teacher accused of being an IWW member, various other antiradical investigations, the Americanization movement, and several strikes and boycotts. The collection contains much more than is reviewed here.

485. Chase, Ray Park (1880–1948). Papers, undated, 1897–1944. 44 boxes.

Chase was an anti-Communist politician who served in Congress, 1933–35. He was defeated in his 1930 run for governor by F-L candidate Floyd B. Olson and spent the 1930s investigating Communist activity in state government. In 1938 he wrote *Are They Communists or Catspaws?*, an attack on alleged Communist influence in the F-LP, which spawned a series of counterattacks in pamphlet form. Information on radicalism is scattered throughout the correspondence/miscellaneous papers files and the subject files and includes items about government ownership, the F-LP, 1925–38, the Union party, the Workers Alliance, and various individuals, such as Elmer Benson, Joseph A. A. Burnquist, Floyd B. Olson, and Magnus Johnson.

486. Christensen, Otto Augustus (1851–1918). Family papers, 1854–1964. 3 boxes.

Oscar A. Christensen, Otto's son, was secretary-treasurer of the Cooperative Union Activities. The collection contains his correspondence and papers regarding various farm organizations, 1934–41, including the Farmers' Union, the Farm Holiday Assn., the factional conflict within the Farmers' Union, and the formation of the Cooperative Union Activities group.

487. Christgau, Victor A. (1894–   ). Papers, 1922–68. 1 box.

Christgau was a F-L politician from Mower County who served in the state senate, 1927–29, and Congress, 1929–33. His papers document his political campaigns and his desire to keep Communists out of the F-LP.

488. Citizens Alliance of Minneapolis. Records, undated, 1903–53. 22 rolls microfilm.

The Citizens Alliance was a group of conservative

businessmen and politicians, who worked to prevent unionization in Minneapolis. The collection is organized by topical subject files and contains mostly newspaper clippings and pamphlets.

489. The Committee of 48 (Minnesota State Central Committee). Papers, 1920–24. 1 box.

The committee was organized to establish a national progressive party. The collection includes correspondence regarding fund raising, candidates for offices, and relations with other third parties, such as the F-LP and the NPL.

490. Cotton, Donald R. (1883–). Papers, undated, 1915–19, 1925. 3 boxes.

Cotton directed the Ramsey County branch of the Commission of Public Safety, an organization that sought to repress and prohibit radical political activity during World War I. He also chaired the commission's War Inventions and Research Committee. The collection includes correspondence with Theodore Roosevelt regarding the influence of the NPL in Minnesota and the Dakotas.

491. Cramer, Robley Dungleson (1884–1966), and Family. Papers, 1887–1966. 6 boxes.

Cramer edited the *Minneapolis Labor Review,* 1913–63. He was associated with the Socialist party and a member of the Upholsters' Union. His papers contain information about the Socialist party, Communist party, the F-LP, the DFL, the Minneapolis Central Labor Union, the AFL-CIO, the Upholsterers' Union, and the Citizens Alliance. Included are materials about the *Cramer vs. Citizens Alliance* libel trial, 1932–37.

492. Davis, Ida Blehart (1895–1970). Papers, undated, 1958, 1967–68. 8 items. Restricted in part.

Davis was a St. Paul social worker. Her papers contain articles written by her, as well as many other people, including Meridel Le Sueur, Irene Paull, Oscar Christensen, Susie Stageberg, Clarence Hathaway, Carl Ross, John Bernard, Donald Pierson, and a variety of other authors all writing on labor and agricultural topics.

493. Davis, Sam K. (1899–1968). Papers, 1919–80. 4 boxes.

Davis was a labor activist, editor of *Midwest Labor,* and for many years an active member of the Com-

munist party. His papers include subject files, correspondence concerning the Communist party, Communist activities within the CIO, civil rights, Henry Wallace, and individual labor unions.

494. Day, Frank Arah (1855–1928). Papers, 1889–1928. 5 boxes.

Day was the editor and publisher of the *Fairmont Daily Sentinel,* 1910–28, and held a variety of elected and appointed public offices, first as a Republican and later as a Democrat. His papers include information on the growth of the F-LP.

495. Day, Vincent Alpheus (1886–1945). Papers, 1906–45. 3 boxes, 29 oversize items.

Day was a socialist in his early years and became a F-L activist. He was Governor Olson's private secretary, 1931–35. His papers provide substantial information on the farm depression, the Bank Holiday, the 1934 political campaign, the 1934 Minneapolis truck drivers' strike, third-party movements in the 1930s, and the activities of the Communist party. Included is correspondence from Selden Rodman, editor of *Common Sense,* which discusses the 1934 murder of Walter Liggett, editor of the *Midwest American,* and from Robert Happ about the Strutwear Knitting Co. and Flour City Ornamental Iron Works strikes in Minneapolis in 1935. The Happ correspondence discusses the repercussions of Communist activity in these strikes and in the labor movement in general.

496. Deinard, Amos Spencer (1898–1985). Papers, undated, 1911, 1924, 1927, 1956–68. 1 folder.

The collection includes information on the La Follette-Wheeler presidential campaign in Minnesota, 1924, and also contains a brochure charging that there were Communists and IWW members in Olson's government.

497. Democratic-Farmer-Labor State Central Committee. Papers, 1944–[54]. 35 boxes. Restricted.

This collection covers the period 1944–54 and is concentrated mainly on the conflicts within the DFL between Progressive party supporters and the Democratic mainstream, 1948–49. It includes letters, reports, minutes of meetings, clippings, press releases, and committee lists relating to the 1948 campaigns. Issues covered include the controversial endorsement of Truman over Henry Wallace,

Humphrey's campaign for the U.S. Senate and his problems with Progressive party supporters, and the DFL court case in which Progressive party supporters attempted to declare the presidential electors chosen at the Brainerd convention illegal. Also of note is correspondence from 1946–47 concerning the defeat of left-wing activists at the Young DFL convention in Minneapolis.

498. Dispatch-Pioneer Press, St. Paul. Papers, 1862–1948. 4 boxes.

The papers contain correspondence, clippings, pamphlets, and other printed materials concerning the repression of radical groups around the years of World War I, including transcripts of testimony given to the Commission of Public Safety by Henry Teigan, 1917–18, James Ingalls, 1917, and Arthur Townley, 1917, regarding the organizing activities of the NPL, its affiliation with Socialists, and alleged disloyal activities.

499. Dizard, George E. (1917–), and Family. Papers, 1923–91. 2 boxes.

George E. and Rhoda Levine Dizard of Duluth were active in labor and political movements in northern Minnesota, 1930s–90s. Dizard, business agent for the Diamond Tool Union, Local 18650, was a leader of Henry Wallace's 1948 presidential campaign in northeast Minnesota. Their papers include correspondence, clippings, circulars, and speeches relating to their activities, including correspondence with Elmer Benson, John Bernard, and Irene Paull and materials concerning the Progressive and Communist parties.

500. Drake, Benjamin B. (1880–1961). Equity Cooperative Exchange Papers, 1906–29. 3 boxes.

Drake was a Minneapolis attorney for the Equity Cooperative Exchange, 1907–26. The ECE was a farmers' cooperative-selling agency, which competed directly with the Minneapolis Chamber of Commerce. It was investigated by the Minnesota legislature in 1913, the U.S. Congress in 1914, and the Federal Trade Commission in 1923. It was eventually absorbed by the Farmers' Union. The collection is primarily letters, clippings, manuscripts, printed materials, documents, and reports.

501. Duluth CIO Industrial Council Papers, 1937–56. 2 boxes.

The collection includes minutes of regular meetings and executive board meetings and miscellaneous papers.

502. Duluth Federated Trades and Labor Assembly. Papers, 1892–1942. 10 boxes.

The collection consists of general correspondence and meeting minutes of the assembly, which was an affiliate of the AFL. Boxes 4 and 5 include items on the Socialist party of Duluth, the Working People's NPL of Minnesota, and correspondence relating to a resolution (found in volume 7 of their minutes) to restore citizenship to Eugene V. Debs.

503. Dunn, Roy Emery (1886–1985). Papers, 1927–66. 11 boxes.

Dunn, a resort owner and Republican politician from Otter Tail County, served in the Minnesota House of Representatives, 1925–67, where he was a leader of the house conservatives. His papers include information about the F-LP and its Republican opponents.

504. Enkel, Kenneth J. (1916–). Papers, 1947–58. 3 boxes. (IHRC)

Enkel, a lawyer, defended aliens in the Upper Midwest who faced deportation under the McCarran-Walter Act. He took such cases on behalf of the Minnesota Committee for the Protection of the Foreign Born. Enkel's papers consist of legal briefs, documents, and correspondence relating to deportation proceedings in the McCarthy era, including the following cases: Taisto A. Elo, Knut E. Heikkinen, Vera Hathaway, Harry Roast, Charles Rowoldt, *Lopez-Hernandez vs. Brownell,* and *Heikkila vs. Barber.*

505. Farm Holiday Association. Collection, 1970–72. 6 in. (Southwest)

The Farm Holiday Assn., created in 1932, mobilized farmer activism by withholding agricultural goods from the market in order to raise farm produce prices. The association organized marches and rallies and publicized the plight of the farmer and their own successful activities. The collection includes research materials, such as notes, research papers, and slides.

506. Farmer-Labor Association of Minnesota, St. Paul. Papers, 1918–48. 8 boxes, 4 vols.

An impressive group of Minnesotans met at the State Capitol in 1937 to lunch and decide the fate of a national third-party effort based on Farmer-Labor and similar groups. Well-known names include John Bosch, standing sixth from left; Walfrid Engdahl, to Bosch's left; Viena Johnson (Hendrickson), seated left; Howard Y. Williams, seated center; and Henry Teigan, seated second from right.

The collection contains information about F-L support of La Follette, patronage under F-L government, tax reforms in Minnesota, relief, collective bargaining, the Minneapolis truck drivers' strike of 1934, the Magnus Johnson Memorial, the merger creating the DFL, Tom Mooney, the F-LP, the American Commonwealth Political Federation, the Farmer-Labor Political Federation, the Socialist party, the Republican party, and a history of the association.

507. Farmer-Labor Federation. "Report of the Farmer-Labor Federation Convention, Richmond Halls, Minneapolis, March 12, 1924." 1 roll filmslides.
The collection includes a declaration of principles and platforms of the F-LP and the constitution of the federation.

508. Finnish Socialist Club, Nashwauk. Papers, 1905–13. 3 folders. In Finnish.
The collection includes the club's account book and minutes of the meetings.

509. Finnish Socialist Federation Chapter, Ely. Records, 1905–66. 1 roll microfilm. In Finnish. (IHRC)
The organization was founded around 1910 as a

chapter of the Finnish Socialist Federation. In the Socialist-Communist split of 1920, the Ely group went with the Communists and became a chapter of the Finnish Workers Federation. Records consist of meeting minutes.

510. Finnish Socialist Federation Chapter, Markham. Records, 1911–31. 1 folder. In Finnish. (IHRC)
The Markham organization was a chapter of the Finnish Socialist Federation. After the Socialist-Communist split in 1920, the Markham group continued with the Socialists. Records consist of meeting minutes.

511. Finnish Workers Club, Inc., Hibbing. Papers, 1902–61. 2 folders. In Finnish.
The collection contains miscellaneous papers, minutes of the meetings, 1942–61, and an account book, 1902–06.

512. Finnish Workers Club, Nashwauk. Papers, 1930–35. 1 vol. In Finnish.
The collection contains the minutes of meetings.

513. Finnish Workers' Federation of the United States

(New York). Records, 1910–67. 2 boxes. In Finnish, some English. (IHRC)

> The federation was organized in 1927 and incorporated in New York City in 1932. It was the political, cultural, and educational organization of Finnish-American Communists and actively supported militant labor unions, farmers' organizations, the cooperative movement, and the unemployed movement. In 1941 the federation joined the International Workers' Order as the Finnish American Mutual Aid Society. Records of the federation include minutes, corporate documents, correspondence, financial records, and reference material. Also included are financial statements of the People's Voice Cooperative Publishing Co. in New York Mills.

514. Finnish Workers' Society. "Kehitys" Archive (Cloquet). Records, 1911–39. 4 rolls microfilm. In Finnish. (IHRC)

> This Cloquet organization was founded in 1903 and in 1906 joined the Socialist party and the Finnish Socialist Federation. During the 1914 schism between the Socialists and the IWW, the group withdrew from all national organizations and became an independent workers' society. Records of the society consist of financial statements, minutes, membership lists, and play scripts.

515. Fosseen, Carrie Secelia Jorgens (1875–1963). Papers, 1914–51. 1 box, 1 roll microfilm.

> Fosseen was an active member of the Republican party. Her papers include speeches against radical political movements of the 1920s and 1930s.

516. Foster, Ellery A. (1906?–). Papers, 1934–77. 1 box.
> Foster was director of research and education for the International Woodworkers of America (CIO), 1945–48. The collection contains information on the lumber industry, conservation, and labor, plus articles written by Foster.

517. Frank, Walter Malte (1893–). Papers, undated, 1922–60. 1 box.

> Frank, an immigrant from Sweden, participated in the IWW strikes of 1913–15 in Washington and Oregon. He moved to Minnesota in 1915, joined the Wood, Wire, and Metal Lathers International Union, Local 190, and became a left-wing leader of the Minneapolis Central Labor Union. The collection includes information about the Free Tom Mooney Committee, the early F-L organization, and many manuscripts of speeches.

518. Frankel, Hiram D. (1873–1931). Papers, 1873–1931. 18 boxes, 1 oversize folder.

> Frankel was a St. Paul lawyer affiliated with many civic organizations, including the Anti-Socialist League in 1918, of which he was president of the investigating committee. Box 7 of the collection contains information on the league.

519. Frankel, Hiram D. (1873–1931). "Report on Labor Disturbances in Northern Minnesota, December 1919–January 6, 1920." 26 p.

> The report is an account of the strike at International Falls on the Minnesota, Dakota, and Western Railway, activities of the IWW, and efforts at mediation.

520. Fraser, Donald Mackay (1924–). Papers, 1944–85. 495 boxes. Restricted.

> Fraser was DFL state senator, 1955–62, U.S. Representative, 1965–79, and mayor of Minneapolis, 1980–94. He was part of the liberal anti-Communist movement, which expelled Communists from the DFL party. He was active in many DFL and civic organizations. Box 2 contains information on the Young DFL convention and caucuses of 1947–49 and on the Henry Wallace campaign of 1947–48.

521. Freeman, Orville L. (1918–). Papers, 1903–76. 33 boxes, 1 roll microfilm.

> Freeman became active in F-L politics in 1941 as part of the liberal anti-Communist movement, which expelled Communists from the DFL party. He served as a DFL governor, 1955–61, and as U.S. secretary of agriculture, 1961–69. His papers include information on Americans for Democratic Action, 1947–48; the Henry Wallace campaign, 1947–48; photographs of ads for rallies for the Communist party, 1948; newspaper clippings from *Action*, the newspaper of the Communist party; copies of the Communist publication, *New Leader*, 1948; speeches from his 1954 gubernatorial campaign; and correspondence with Hubert Humphrey. (Note: See also Freeman's papers in the Governors' Papers, State Archives.)

522. General Drivers, Helpers and Inside Workers Union, Local 574 (Minneapolis). Minneapolis Teamsters Strike, 1934: Selected Documents, 1928–41. 1 roll microfilm. Originals in the Library of Social History, New York, N.Y.

Correspondence, telegrams, clippings, legal documents, and broadsides documenting the strike. Selected by Farrell Dobbs, former secretary-treasurer of Local 574, from his papers.

523. Genis, Sander David (1895–). Papers, undated, 1933–65. 3 folders.

Genis was a Russian immigrant who became president of the Minnesota CIO in 1942 and served as vice-president of the Amalgamated Clothing Workers of America, 1946–75. The collection consists of speeches, reports, and other material concerning his activities in the labor movement.

524. Gilbert, Joseph (1865–1956). Papers, 1886–1954. 1 box, 6 oversize items.

Gilbert was a socialist, a NPL organizer, and a leader in the cooperative movement. He founded and edited the *Midland Cooperator* in Minneapolis, 1933–53. His papers contain materials on the cooperative movement, socialism, and his F-L campaign for Congress. Also included are copies of F-LP platforms, 1936–43, Elmer Benson's speeches on cooperatives, and clippings from the *Midland Cooperator.*

525. Gillmor, Frank H. (1875–). Papers, 1910–48. 1 box.

The collection contains the business records of the Virginia and Rainy Lake Lumber Co., 1910–28, which refer to the IWW.

526. Goldman, Rose (1901?–75), and Samuel Goldman (1900–77). "Aunt Rose" and "Uncle Sam," 1975, 1977. 22 p., 53 p. Restricted in part.

The file consists of two memoirs written by their nephew, Daniel J. Elazar. Rose Goldman was an active Zionist, Socialist, and labor supporter in Minneapolis. Samuel, a social worker, was active in the F-LP and the Minneapolis Jewish community.

527. Gray, James, and Family. Papers, 1862–1960. 10 boxes.

Gray was a writer, professor, and reporter. His papers include superficial interviews with George Lawson, head of the AFL; George B. Leonard, a prominent Socialist party member, 1910–20; and Maurice Visscher, a medical school professor and socialist.

528. Great Northern Railway Company, St. Paul. Records, 1874–1970. Ca. 4,800 cu.ft. Restricted in part.

The Great Northern Railway's records contain documentation of the company's reaction to the labor movement and labor strife, including its use of detective agencies to undermine workers' attempts at organization, its actions against strikes, and losses incurred by strikes. There is also information concerning Americanization, the Citizens Alliance, and the IWW. Most of these materials concerning labor conflicts are located in the subject files of the Presidents Office, the Offices of the Vice-President of Operations, or the General Manager. (Note: The Minnesota Historical Society holds the complete archives of the company. For guidance in using this collection, see Karen Wilson and John Wickre, "A Survey of Minnesota Labor Materials in the Papers of the Great Northern Railway and Northern Pacific Railroad Companies in the Minnesota Historical Society," at the Research Center reference desk.)

529. Hagen, Harold Christian (1901–57). Papers, 1923–57. 43 boxes.

Hagen served as secretary to F-L Congressman Richard T. Buckler, 1934–42, whom he succeeded in Congress in 1943. He was reelected in 1944, this time as a Republican, and he served until 1955. The collection contains correspondence and other materials concerning the American Cooperative Alliance (an organization supporting government ownership of the railroads), Communist influence in the F-LP, various F-L campaigns, the DFL merger, Henry Wallace, Elmer Benson, the proceedings of the House Un-American Activites Committee, the Federal Loyalty Commission, and other anti-Communist organizations.

530. Haines, Lynn (1876–1929). Papers, 1909–31. 61 boxes.

Haines was an editor of *Searchlight on Congress,* a publication of the National Voters' League, during the 1920s. The collection includes correspondence with many prominent people interested in the league, voting records, clippings, and other data on congressmen. There is mention of the Committee of 48 and other liberal programs.

531. Hall, Douglas. Papers, ca. 1930–50. 41 boxes.

The papers include information about the labor movement in the 1940s, specifically the United Electrical, Radio, and Machine Workers, Locals 1140 and 1145, which were expelled from the CIO in 1949.

532. Hall, Emanuel George (1865–1938). Papers, 1885–1937. 3 rolls microfilm.

Hall was a Minnesota labor leader and cigar maker. He was an organizer for the AFL in the early 1900s and in 1916 was involved in the Labor Forward Movement in northern Minnesota. The collection includes information on the attitude of organized labor toward World War I, the League of Nations, the Working People's NPL, and the NPL. The collection documents his efforts to organize workers on the Mesabi Iron Range.

533. Hapgood, Powers (1899–1949). Letters and journal, September–November 1920. 3 folders. Photocopies. Literary rights reserved. Originals in Lilly Library, Indiana University, Bloomington.

Hapgood kept a journal and sent letters home while he was working and traveling through Minnesota, North Dakota, and Montana. The purpose of his trip was to become acquainted with the labor movement, particularly among semiskilled and unskilled workers. He worked on the iron range for the Oliver Mining Co. near Hibbing and with the Northern Pacific Railroad in North Dakota. He joined the United Mineworkers of America, Local 1727, in Montana. He wrote about his discussions with laborers, labor activists, and members of the IWW. He became active in the Socialist party and helped found the CIO.

534. Harju, Walter A. (1900–   ). Papers, ca. 1929–73. 3 boxes. (IHRC)

Harju, a writer, carpenter, and historian, worked for the WPA Federal Writers' Project in Minnesota during the 1930s. Harju wrote about Finns in America and Minnesota, the cooperative movement, and trade unionism. He served as California correspondent for *Työmies-Eteenpäin,* Superior. His papers include correspondence, speeches, articles, oral histories, and information by or about *Työmies-Eteenpäin* and the Workers and Farmers Cooperative Unity Alliance.

535. Hathaway, Clarence A. (1894–1963). Papers, 1928–40. 1 box.

Hathaway began his career as a St. Paul tool and die maker. Originally a Socialist, he became one of the organizers and charter members of the American Communist party in 1921. He was expelled from the St. Paul Trades and Labor Assembly in 1924 because of his Communist party affiliation. Hathaway edited the *Daily Worker* in New York, 1934–39. He was expelled from the Communist party in 1940 and readmitted to the party in the 1950s. He worked as a business agent for the United Electrical, Radio and Machine Workers, 1946–49. The collection includes transcripts of speeches, many of which focus on the conflict among Socialist groups in America over the United Front policy of the Communist party, the effect of Hitler's rise to power on the Socialist and Communist movements in Germany, freedom of the press, his objections to Zionism, world peace, religion and Communism, and general lectures on Communist doctrine.

536. Hawkins, Oscar Ferdinand (1872–1964), and Family. Papers, 1888–1963. 11 boxes.

Hawkins was active in F-L and Socialist parties in the 1920s. In 1933 he formally joined the Socialist party. He was an unsuccessful candidate for mayor in Minneapolis, governor in Minnesota, and president of the United States. His papers contain materials from and about the F-L, Socialist, Communist, Progressive, and various other left-wing parties and groups formed during the 1930s and 1940s, including campaign materials from these parties, letters to the editors of various newspapers on political topics, Socialist Labor party news clippings on the Minneapolis truck drivers' strike of 1934, and many pamphlets and newspapers from radical organizations.

537. Hawkins, Oscar Ferdinand (1872–1964), and Madge Ytrehus Hawkins (1883–1969). Papers, 1892–1972. 2 boxes.

This collection supplements the preceding collection of the Hawkinses' papers. It includes Madge Hawkins's papers and contains materials about the Hennepin County Farmer-Labor Women's Club, 1937–38, and the 1948 Henry Wallace campaign. Also included is a large selection of radical pamphlets.

538. Hendrickson, Paul Hiram (1892–1979). Papers, 1916–20, 1965, 1967. 1 box.

Hendrickson, an employee of the city of Minneapolis, was active in the Socialist party in 1916. His papers include personal letters to his fiancée and wife, Isabel Austin, in which he writes about his activities and his perspective on union problems. He mentions the Minnesota Commission of Public Safety. Hendrickson married Viena Pasanen Johnson in 1953.

539. Hendrickson, Viena Rakel Pasanen Johnson (1898–1980), and Family. Papers, 1892–1980. 20 boxes.
Viena Hendrickson, the daughter of Finnish immigrants, grew up in northern Minnesota. She was active in various F-L organizations during the 1930s and was the F-L candidate for state senate in the 57th District (Duluth) in 1934. She was the first woman to serve on the Minnesota State Teachers College Board, 1937–41. She was also active in the International Ladies' Garment Workers Union, 1952–53, the Women's International League for Peace and Freedom, 1936–71, and the DFL party. Her papers contain much information relating to these organizations and her activities in them, including materials on the investigations into her Communist affiliations, 1945–49. She married Paul Hiram Hendrickson in 1953.

540. Hibbing Central Labor Union, Hibbing. Papers, undated, 1937–59. 1 box.
The collection includes newspaper clippings and minutes of meetings, 1937–59 (with a gap, 1953–55). There is information on the organization of the group in 1916.

541. Hibbing Finnish Workers' Club. Records, 1935–74. 2 folders. In Finnish, some English. (IHRC)
Records consist of minutes and a ledger of accounts.

542. Howard, Asher (1877–1945), comp. A Collection of Letters and Printed Material Relating to the Nonpartisan League and Other Organizations, 1905–20. 2 boxes.
Asher was a state representative from Hennepin County, 1917–22.

543. Humphrey, Hubert H. (1911–78). Papers, 1945–78. Ca. 2,400 boxes. Restricted in part.
Humphrey played a key role in the liberal anti-Communist movement that expelled Communists from the DFL party. He was Minneapolis mayor, 1945–48, U.S. Senator, 1949–64, 1971–78, and U.S. vice-president, 1965–69. Humphrey's papers from the 1940s and 1950s, in particular, contain much information

on organized labor and its relationship to third-party political groups, such as the Communist and Socialist parties. Also of interest are campaign materials. For a fuller description of the papers, see *Hubert H. Humphrey Papers: A Summary Guide, Including the Papers of Muriel Humphrey Brown* (St. Paul: Minnesota Historical Society, 1983), 35 p.

544. Hurley, Helen Angela (1897–1975), comp. The John Ireland Collection, 1838–1959. 9 boxes, 18 rolls microfilm.
Collection contains information about the antiradicalism of the Catholic church. It includes a copy of *Socialism's Menace* by John Ireland, archbishop of St. Paul, from the early 1900s.

545. Hursh, Morris (1906–). Interview, Oct. 15, 1968. 19 p.
Hursh served as executive secretary for Governors Floyd Olson, Hjalmar Petersen, and Elmer Benson, 1931–39. The interview details the governors' different approaches to politics, Olson's relationship with Franklin Roosevelt, the conflicts within the F-LP, and Benson's appointment to the U.S. Senate in 1935. Interviewed by Lila M. Johnson.

546. Iron Ranges Industrial Union Council, CIO, Hibbing. Minute Book, 1937–50. 1 roll microfilm.
The council had representatives from all three iron ranges (Mesabi, Cuyuna, and Vermilion), and its books contain information on routine business, the Workers Alliance, strikes, and its affiliation with the Farmer-Labor Assn.

547. Jackson County Farm Holiday Association. Records, 1932–34. 31 items. (Southwest)
Minutes of meetings, membership items, and other records of the association.

548. Jacobsen, John Melseth (1903–66). Papers, 1935–49, 1962–67. 5 boxes.
Jacobsen was regional and state director of the CIO Political Action Committee and represented CIO labor interests in the state legislature, 1944–48. The collection includes materials on such topics as marine unions, propaganda, labor and work hours, monopoly, organized labor in the Soviet Union, Palestine, anti-Semitism, war veterans, Henry Wallace and the Progressive party, consumer issues, health issues, racial discrimination, collective health care,

voter awareness, unionism, wages, co-ops, taxation, the world food crisis, price controls, workers' compensation, the economic outlook, specific unions, inflation, civil rights, and loyalty.

549. Janney, Semple, Hill Company, Minneapolis. Papers, 1866–1951. 1 box.

These papers from a wholesale hardware firm include a speech entitled, "Capital and Labor—The Rights of the Public," probably given about 1905, that outlines the viewpoint of a businessman toward labor problems and government regulation of industry.

550. Jewish Community Relations Council of Minnesota, Minneapolis. Papers, undated, 1922–67. 63 boxes.

The council investigated the activities of right-wing organizations in Minnesota and elsewhere. The collection contains clippings, correspondence, publications, and reports relating to their investigations of anti-Semitic organizations. Papers are arranged by names of people and organizations or incidents. Includes files concerning Mothers of Minnesota, an antiradical, isolationist organization active from the late 1930s through the end of World War II.

551. Johnson, Magnus (1871–1936). Papers, 1923–41. 11 boxes.

Johnson, an early F-L politician, served in the Minnesota house, 1915–18, and senate, 1919–22, and in the U.S. Congress as Senator, 1923–25, and Representative, 1933–35. His papers include materials about Socialist, NPL, and F-LP activity, 1914–36, and his decision to run for governor against Elmer Benson in 1936. Also included is information on the 1932–36 campaigns.

552. Johnson, Samuel, and Family. Papers, 1882–1980. 3 boxes. In Danish, some English.

Johnson was the Minnesota representative to the National Executive Committee of the Socialist Labor party in the 1910s. The collection contains correspondence and other papers of the Socialist Labor party after 1901, including minutes of party meetings in Minnesota, 1945–48, 1950; organizational files, 1893–1951; financial records, 1894–1948; and printed materials, 1894–1948.

553. Judd, Walter Henry (1898–1994). Papers, 1918, 1942–62. 212 boxes.

Judd, a Republican congressman, 1943–63, opposed U.S. policy in China in the late 1940s. The collection includes materials on the House Un-American Activities Committee, 1940–49; the Institute of Pacific Relations, an alleged Communist-front organization, 1947; the Mundt-Nixon Bill, 1948; and Joseph McCarthy, 1950–51, 1954. This information is found chiefly in boxes 58–59, 103, 145, and 171–172.

554. Kampelman, Max M. (1920–). Papers, 1940–83. 32 boxes. Restricted.

Kampelman was an aide to Senator Hubert Humphrey, 1949–55. His papers include materials from the Humphrey correspondence files on Communism and the DFL in the early 1950s, as well as items relating to Senator Joseph McCarthy and loyalty issues.

555. Kane, Lucile M. "Memorandum of Legal Cases, 1934." 1 p. Complete files are located at the Federal Records Center, Kansas City, Mo.

A list of the files of two cases arising from the Minneapolis truck drivers' strike of 1934.

556. Kaplan, Morris (1869–1959), and Family. Papers, 1924–64. 1 box. Literary rights reserved.

Kaplan was Socialist party candidate for U.S. Senate in 1934. He organized Socialist groups in northern Minnesota and was active in the 1907 iron mine strikes, in which he helped to start commissaries for strikers' families. Later, he helped organize cooperative grocery stores and served as president of the National Cooperative Mercantile Co. of Duluth. The collection consists of correspondence, newspaper clippings, reminiscences, and an autobiographical manuscript. Also included are notes for speeches on Socialism, letters to the editor on Socialism, and various pamphlets and newspapers.

557. Karow, Edward (1884–). Papers, 1917–25. 10 vols.

Karow was an officer in the Minneapolis Civilian Auxiliary, the Home Guard of Minnesota, the National Guard, and the U.S. Army. His papers include information about the use of the Minneapolis Civilian Auxiliary and the Home Guard by the Minnesota Commission of Public Safety during strikes, as well as materials on the suppression of a 1918 Socialist parade by the Minnesota National Guard (on orders from Governor Burnquist).

558. Kellogg, Frank B. (1856–1937). Correspondence and miscellaneous papers, 1890–1942. 51 rolls microfilm.
Kellogg, a Republican, was U.S. Senator, 1917–23, ambassador to Great Britain, 1923–25, and U.S. secretary of state, 1925–29. This collection provides information about politics in Minnesota, including materials on the NPL, the ethnic vote, Robert La Follette, Socialism, U.S. denial of entrance visas to Communists, Communist propaganda activities in the U.S. and Europe, and F-LP politics.

559. Koch, Robert F., to Miss Fitzgibbons. Letter. 1937.
This two-page letter discusses the purpose and work of the American Consumers Union, a group formed to investigate causes and circumstances of particular strikes.

560. Koivisto, Edith Laine (1888–1981). Papers, 1903–81. 21 boxes. In Finnish, some English. (IHRC)
Koivisto immigrated from Finland in 1910. In 1912 she attended Työväen-Opisto (Work People's College) in Duluth. She married Arvid Koivisto, and they settled in Hibbing where Arvid worked for the Hibbing Co-op. Arvid was also an accountant at the Central Cooperative Wholesale in Superior, although he remained a resident of Hibbing. Papers include biographical material on Finnish Americans in Minnesota and records and information about Finnish-American organizations, temperance societies, the Work People's College, and the Central Cooperative Wholesale.

561. Koski, Ernest Theodore (1908–89). Papers, ca. 1950–83. 1 box. In Finnish. (IHRC)
Papers consist of clippings, memorabilia, correspondence, and information on the Työmies Society and *Työmies-Eteenpäin.*

562. Kunze, William Frederick (1872–1962). Papers, 1865–1962. 11 boxes.
Kunze was mayor of Minneapolis, 1929–31, and was involved in many civic organizations, including the Parents and Teachers Council, which brought charges against Minneapolis high-school teacher W. R. Ball for teaching un-American doctrine in the early 1920s. The collection contains information on this investigation.

563. Latchem, Edwin Wilbur (1888–). Papers, 1915–65. 8 items. Carbon copies and photocopies. Originals are in the possession of E. W. Latchem, Sapulpa, Okla.

The collection includes manuscripts and newspaper clippings about the IWW, public reaction to the IWW, and students' interest in the IWW.

564. Lawson, Victor (1871–1960). Biography. 2 p.
Lawson of Kandiyohi County was a F-L state senator, 1927–37. This is a two-page handwritten list of Lawson's achievements, offices, and honors. Lawson edited the *Willmar Tribune* and was active in a wide range of civic organizations.

565. Leach, George E. (1876–1955). "The Personal History of Major General George E. Leach," 1951–52. 1 roll microfilm. 207 p.
Leach was mayor of Minneapolis, 1921–29, 1937–41. This family history and autobiography documents his experiences with the Citizens Alliance and his impressions of his political opponents, including William Anderson, Thomas Van Lear, and William Kunze.

566. Lee, Algernon (1873–1954). Papers, 1890–1915. 55 p. Originals are in the possession of the Tamiment Institute Library, New York.
Lee, originally from St. Paul, was a journalist, socialist writer, and director of the Rand School of Social Science, 1909–54. Includes information about Lee's work in the Populist and Socialist parties and his acquaintanceship with Minneapolis Socialist leader, George B. Leonard.

567. Leekley, Richard. Papers, 1939–40. 1 box.
Leekley was preparing a history of the F-LP. The collection consists of correspondence, including letters from Benjamin Drake, Susie Stageberg, Henry Teigan, Vincent Day, and Ernest Lundeen; interview notes; and a rough draft of the manuscript (7 folders).

568. Lemberg, Lauri (1887–1965). Papers, 1920–68. 3 boxes. In Finnish.
Lemberg, a Finnish immigrant in northern Minnesota, worked as a printer, typesetter, and part-time editor on a variety of newspapers. He was active in the Finnish community in Duluth, particularly the Workers' Opera, which was sponsored by the Finnish Socialist party in Duluth. He edited *Siirtokansan Kalenteri* (Immigrants' Calendar), 1940–61, and wrote articles for *American News, Industrialisti,* and other newspapers. The collection

ARCHIVAL AND MANUSCRIPT COLLECTIONS

consists of copies of plays and a novel by Lemberg, newspaper clippings of his news column and articles about him, and booking ledgers. All papers are in Finnish with no translation except for the obituary and a few sample clippings.

569. Leonard, George B. (1872–1956). Papers, 1876–1957. 11 boxes.

Leonard was an attorney and organizer for the Socialist party of Minneapolis. The collection contains correspondence, printed material, and clippings concerning various liberal political groups, Jewish organizations, peace organizations, and farm groups, including the Socialist party, 1888–1910, the American Civil Liberties Union, 1923–47, and the National Lawyer's Guild, 1936–42. Also included is information on alleged Communist infiltration of the ACLU and the Lawyer's Guild and the prohibition of Communist or Socialist party candidates from appearing on some state ballots. There is also information on various congressional and presidential campaigns.

570. Le Sueur, Arthur (1867–1950). Papers, 1910–54. 14 boxes.

Le Sueur edited a socialist newspaper and practiced law in Minot, N.Dak. In 1917 he moved to St. Paul and became education director of the NPL, although by 1920 he opposed the league's leadership. He served on the Minneapolis school board and was appointed a municipal judge by Governor Elmer Benson in 1937. Marion Le Sueur, his wife, served on the executive board of the F-LP and later as state chairwoman of the DFL. Her association with the DFL ended in 1948 when she backed Henry Wallace's bid for the presidency on the Progressive party ticket. The papers include correspondence related to the Socialist party, 1910–14, the NPL, 1915–24, cooperatives, 1925–29, the Communist party, 1925–34, 1940–47, the Workers Alliance, 1935–39, and the F-LP and the Progressive party, 1945–54. Also included is other printed material concerning the NPL, Elmer Benson, 1936–47, Le Sueur's political campaigns, Roger Rutchik, 1941–45, Independent Voters of Minnesota, 1946–47, the case of Job Wells Brinton (a former league official) against the NPL, 1919–22, and various deportation cases.

571. Le Sueur, Meridel (1900–   ). Papers, 1906–86. 20 boxes. Restricted until 2012.

Le Sueur is an author, feminist, and radical political activist. Her papers include correspondence, clippings, and other printed material relating to her family and her career. The inventory has general listings of box contents only.

572. Lewis, Russell K. (1901–83). Papers, 1925–66. 22 boxes.

Lewis, a leader in the Minnesota cooperative movement, helped establish Group Health in 1942. The collection contains much information on Group Health and some files belonging to George W. Jacobsen, senator, friend, and business associate of Lewis, including Jacobsen's personal files about the F-LP, Americans for Democratic Action, the League for Independent Action, the F-L Political Federation, and the American Commonwealth Political Federation. Also included are files on the WPA Project on Cooperatives, 1933–37, which Lewis headed.

573. Lind, John (1854–1930). Papers, 1870–1912, 1917–33. 12 boxes.

Lind, a Republican, served in the U.S. House, 1887–93, and as governor, 1899–1901, on the Democratic-People's party ticket. He represented Hennepin County in the state house, 1903–05. He was supported by a loose coalition of silver Republicans, William Jennings Bryant Democrats, and Populists. Lind worked for the election of Woodrow Wilson in 1912 and thereafter supported the Democratic party. He was a member of the Minnesota Commission of Public Safety. His papers include minutes of the meetings of the Minnesota Commission of Public Safety and transcripts of the 1917 hearings of the Minnesota House of Representatives Committee on Labor and Labor Legislation on the topic of IWW unrest in northern Minnesota.

574. Lindbergh, Charles Augustus, Sr. (1858–1924), and Family. Papers, 1808–1985. 13 boxes.

Lindbergh was a progressive Republican congressman, 1907–17, who opposed U.S. entry into World War I. In 1918 he ran unsuccessfully as the NPL candidate for governor. His papers include correspondence concerning World War I, the NPL, the Russian Revolution of 1917, capitalism, Communism, Robert La Follette, and the IWW. Additional materials include information about the F-LP and the NPL.

60

575. Lippincott, Benjamin Evans (1902–88). Papers, 1929–46. 1 box. (Uarch)

Lippincott was a professor of political science at the University of Minnesota, 1929–71. His papers include threatening letters written to Lippincott in 1935 concerning his controversial political views and Lippincott's 1940 letter to economics professor Emerson P. Schmidt in which he defended his sympathetic views of socialism.

576. Lockhart, Andrew Francis (1891–1964). Papers, undated, 1920–64. 2 folders.

Lockhart edited the *Minnesota Union Advocate,* 1931–56. In the collection are some of his editorials and other political writings.

577. Lommen, George H. (1895–1942). Papers, 1922–42. 1 vol.

Lommen was a F-L politician from St. Louis County. He served in the Minnesota house, 1925–27, and senate, 1927–41. The collection consists of newspaper clippings about Lommen.

578. Lovely, Clinton W. (1894–). Papers, 1920–67. 1 box.

Lovely edited the *Minnesota Leader* and was active in the F-LP. The papers include booklets, campaign literature, some correspondence, speeches by Floyd Olson and Elmer Benson, and an affidavit concerning charges of Communism, which were brought against Lovely by the *Minneapolis Journal.*

579. Lowenthal, Max. Papers, ca. 1900–70. 91 p. (Uarch)

Lowenthal wrote *Federal Bureau of Investigation,* a book critical of the FBI. His papers include notes and drafts of the book and research materials on civil liberties and the Joseph McCarthy era.

580. McCarthy, Eugene Joseph (1916–). Papers, 1948–89. 412 boxes. Restricted.

McCarthy, a DFLer, served in the U.S. House, 1949–59, and U.S. Senate, 1959–71. His papers include materials on Communism, 1950–51, 1954, government seizure of railroads, 1951, socialized medicine, 1950, Americanism, 1953–54, cooperatives, 1953–54, the labor movement, and the House Un-American Activities Committee.

581. MacKinnon, George Edward (1906–). Papers, 1919–60. 26 boxes.

MacKinnon served as a Republican in the Minnesota house, 1935–42, and in the U.S. House, 1947–49. He was appointed the U.S. district attorney for Minnesota in 1953 and investigated labor racketeering. His papers include information on Americans for Democratic Action, Communism, the Subversive Activities Control Act, Alger Hiss, Joseph McCarthy, Henry Wallace, Peter J. Warhol, and Luther Youngdahl, as well as various pamphlets.

582. MacMahon, William (1889–1957). Papers, 1920–55. 2 boxes.

MacMahon worked with the Ramsey and Dakota County Citizens Alliance, 1922–28, and the St. Paul Committee on Industrial Relations, 1934–57. The collection is useful in understanding the position of management and conservative companies with regard to the labor movement. The materials cover such topics as the strike at the Andrew Schoch Grocery, St. Paul, and the use of the Floyd M. Andrews Detective Service during the strike. There is also information on the Citizens Alliance and anti-Communist pamphlets by the National Association of Manufacturers, the National Industrial Council, and Standard Oil.

583. Mahoney, William (1869–1952). Papers, 1890–1952. 2 boxes.

Mahoney was a St. Paul labor leader, politician, and mayor. Early in his career he belonged to the Socialist party, but later became anti-Communist and anti-Socialist. He founded the *Minnesota Union Advocate* and was one of the founders of the Working People's NPL and the Farmer-Labor Assn. He was the regional director of the National Labor Relations Board, 1935–36. His papers contain information on his association with Socialists, the decision of the St. Paul Trades and Labor Assembly to purchase the *Minnesota Union Advocate,* on the F-LP and Farmer-Labor Assn., the St. Paul Trades and Labor Assembly's (and Mahoney's) decision to withdraw from the Farmer-Labor Assn., and on the Communist influence in the F-LP and Farmer-Labor Assn. Also included are materials on the Minnesota Commission of Public Safety, Farmer-Labor associations, the Working People's NPL, and the Citizens Alliance.

584. Manahan, James (1866–1932), and Family. Papers, 1883–1935. 10 boxes.

Manahan was a progressive Republican lawyer who was interested in the problems of farmers and involved in the cooperative farm movement. He was a personal friend of William Jennings Bryant and Robert La Follette, Sr. The collection includes an article about the NPL, written by Kathryn Manahan (James's daughter), and legal documents related to a free-speech case during World War I. There are newspaper clippings about the Pullman Co. and American Express cases in which Manahan had a role.

585. Mattson, Theodor Gustaf (1892–   ). Papers, 1921–81. 1 folder.

Mattson was a laborer from Little Falls. This collection includes a 1921 IWW membership booklet containing a record of his dues payments and a newspaper clipping on his early career.

586. Meighen, Thomas J. (1855–1936), and Family. Papers, 1846–1918. 26 boxes.

Meighen was a leader in the Greenback party, Farmers' Alliance, and People's party. He also ran a store in Forestville. This collection is primarily store records, but boxes 2 and 16 include clippings on the third-party movement.

587. Meighen, Thomas J. (1855–1936), and Family. Papers, 1830s–1980s. 43 boxes.

This is a second collection of Meighen Papers. It includes information on the People's party, the F-LP, Charles Lindbergh, Sr., and Magnus Johnson.

588. Melby, John O. (1866–1944). Papers, 1928–44. 1 box.

Melby, a resident of Oklee, served as a F-L representative in the Minnesota house, 1927–43. He was interested in public welfare and health care. The papers focus on his work in developing a statewide program for care of tuberculosis patients who were discharged from sanatoriums.

589. Mesaba and Vermilion Worker's Club, Virginia. Papers, 1931–51. 4 folders. In Finnish.

Minutes of meetings, 1934–51. Some correspondence and financial information included.

590. Minneapolis Social Science Study Club. Papers, 1936–59. 1 box.

The club was a discussion group devoted to a variety of political, economic, and cultural topics, such as the merger of the Democratic and F-L parties. The records contain the minutes and cash books of the club and include many references to Socialism and Communism at home and abroad. Some of the minutes include summaries of the speaker's ideas.

591. Minnesota. Department of Labor and Industry. Biennial Reports, 1888–1988. 2 boxes. (State Archives)

These reports, which were submitted to the governor and the legislature, concern the general condition of labor and industry. They contain background on labor legislation, strikes and lockouts, and working conditions. (Note: Consult the State Archives inventories for additional divisions of the Department of Labor and Industry that may have further information.)

592. Minnesota. Department of Labor and Industry. Correspondence and Miscellaneous Records, 1907–24. 5 boxes. (State Archives)

Information on strikes, disputes and regulations, and safety conditions. (Note: Consult the State Archives inventories for additional divisions of the Department of Labor and Industry that may have further information.)

593. Minnesota. Governor. Records of Governors Floyd B. Olson, Hjalmar Petersen, and Elmer A. Benson, 1932–38. 48 boxes, 5 folders. (State Archives)

These are the official state papers of the F-L governors. They contain correspondence and clippings concerning various strikes and labor organizations, such as the 1933 Hormel strike, the Minneapolis truck drivers' strike in 1934, the Farm Holiday Assn. movement, and the unemployed demonstration at the Capitol, among others. Included are telegrams to the governors requesting militias to control strikers, letters from letter-writing campaigns of the International Labor Defense, the Communist party, and others, and many letters from the general public responding, positively and negatively, to the governors' handling of labor conflict. (Note: Researchers should also consult the papers of the other governors in the State Archives, which contain similar items of interest. Complete inventories for each governor's papers in the State Archives are available. See also the personal papers of the governors in the Manuscripts Collections and Jerry Flower, "A Survey of the State Archives: A Listing of Radical/Labor/Farm Movement Materials in the Minnesota Governors' Papers, 1931–1942.")

594. Minnesota Farmers' Union, St. Paul. Records, 1939–40.

Songbooks, membership cards, and information about social gatherings.

595. Minnesota Federal Writers' Project. Annals of Minnesota, 1849–1942. 45 rolls microfilm.

The Federal Writers' Project was established in 1935 as a part of the WPA to find work for unemployed writers. The Annals of Minnesota was intended to create a comprehensive reference file of historical information transcribed from articles published in Minnesota newspapers. Apparently the survey did not include the radical press. However, reel 44 includes a report from the 1913 *New Ulm Brown County Journal* on a series of lectures on socialism, the first of which "gave the usual arguments" for a socialist government. Also, the *St. Paul Pioneer Press* on Jan. 12, 1922, reported that Nels Nelson, a conservative labor leader, was elected president of the MTLA, the first nonradical president in a while. Franklyn Hynes, a radical, declined reelection.

596. Minnesota Finnish American Family Histories. Collection, ca. 1860–1984. 9 boxes, 154 cassette tapes. (IHRC)

In 1979 the Minnesota Finnish American Family History Project conducted by Carl Ross and Velma Doby began to document the personal histories and experiences of Finnish Americans. The collection contains genealogies, family documents, photographs, and oral histories. Includes material on political and social history.

597. Minnesota Woman Suffrage Association. Records, undated, 1894–1923. 18 rolls microfilm.

The records refer to letters received from the Socialist party and the Minnesota Commission of Public Safety.

598. Munkeby, Elling (1883–). Papers, 1930–55, 1965. 3 folders.

Munkeby was St. Louis County chief jailer, a member of the Duluth City and County Employees Local 66, and president of the Minnesota Council of City and County Employees. The papers include correspondence, clippings, and other printed materials on the labor movement in Duluth, the F-LP, and the American Federation of State, County, and Municipal Employees (AFSCME).

599. Nashwauk Finnish Socialist Chapter and Related Organizations, Nashwauk. Records, 1906–53. 4 boxes. In Finnish. (IHRC)

The organization was affiliated with the Finnish Socialist Federation until 1924, when it changed its name to the Nashwauk Workers' Party Chapter. In 1925 the Workers' party abolished its ethnic chapters, and Nashwauk Finns founded a local Finnish Workers' Assn. In 1932 the name was changed again to the Finnish Workers' Educational Society. In 1908 the women of the original Socialist Club organized a sewing circle, which existed as a women's auxiliary throughout the various name changes of the parent organization. In 1929 the auxiliary became the Nashwauk Finnish Women's Cooperative Guild. Records consist of 22 ledgers reflecting organizational activity.

600. National Nonpartisan League. Membership, Speech and Newspaper Files, undated, 1916–28. 19 rolls microfilm.

Reels 1–17 are specific to Minnesota. The collection includes membership files (by state and town), 1916–18, booster files, 1916–18, convention delegates file, 1918–20, women's clubs membership files, 1921 or 1922, speech files, 1918–21, *Minnesota Leader* subscription files, 1923–25, and National Service Bureau Files, 1918–20. For more information on NPL materials, see Patrick K. Coleman and Charles R. Lamb, comps., *The Nonpartisan League: An Annotated Bibliography, 1915–22* (St. Paul: Minnesota Historical Society Press, 1985).

601. Nelson, Knute (1843–1923). Papers, undated, 1861–1924. 82 boxes.

Nelson was a Republican state senator, a U.S. Congressman, 1883–89, governor, 1893–95, and U.S. Senator, 1895–1923. His papers deal primarily with political and legislative affairs. They contain unsympathetic materials on Robert La Follette, Arthur Townley, the IWW, the Tom Mooney case, the USSR, and bolshevism. Also included is information on agitation both for and against government ownership of railroads.

602. Nonpartisan League. Printed Materials, undated, 1910–28. 4 rolls microfilm.

The collection consists primarily of pamphlets, newspaper clippings, and books.

603. Nordskog, Andrae B. (1885–). Papers, undated, 1919–64. 2 boxes.

Nordskog was a musician and the 1932 vice-presidential candidate of the Liberty party, which called for government ownership of all banks. His papers include information about the Liberty party and the America First Assn. Also included are issues of the *Bugle Call,* the newspaper of the Liberty party.

604. Northeast Neighborhood House, Minneapolis. Papers, 1889–1961. 37 boxes.

Neighborhood House was established by social reformers, Robbins and Catheryne Cooke Gilman, in 1914 to educate community members about childrens' health and hygiene and other social issues. The papers are concerned primarily with social work and youth organizations, including the Young Communist League of Minnesota.

605. Northern Pacific Railroad Company, St. Paul. Records, 1861–1970. Ca. 9,000 cu. ft. Restricted in part.

The Northern Pacific's records contain documentation of the company's reaction to the labor movement and labor strife, including its use of detective agencies to undermine workers' attempts at organization, its actions against strikes, and losses incurred by strikes. There is also information concerning socialism, the Citizens Alliance, the IWW, and the CIO. Materials concerning radical activity and labor conflicts are located in the subject files of the president's office, the offices of the vice-president of operations, or the general manager. (Note: The Minnesota Historical Society holds the complete archives of the company. For guidance in using this collection, see Karen Wilson and John Wickre, "A Survey of Minnesota Labor Materials in the Papers of the Great Northern Railway and Northern Pacific Railroad Companies in the Minnesota Historical Society," at the Research Center reference desk.)

606. O'Donnell, Michael Charles, and Family. Papers, 1883–87, 1911–76. 3 boxes.

Box 1 includes a booklet of newspaper clippings kept by Colonel Charles A. Green during the Minneapolis truck drivers' strike of 1934.

607. Oliver Iron Mining Company, Duluth. Papers, 1901–30. 5 boxes.

The Oliver Iron Mining Co., one of the largest mining companies on the iron range, was the target of several bitter strikes. Its papers include information about Americanization, 1916–20, community affairs, 1903–25, and contributions to local churches, 1902–21, made with the hope of forestalling radical tendencies among workers.

608. Olson, Floyd B. (1891–1936). Papers, 1923–36. 4 boxes.

Papers contain press releases and speeches dating from Olson's term as Minnesota's first F-L governor, 1931–36, arranged alphabetically by subject. Also included is some material on the Farmer-Labor Assn., correspondence and speeches about state relief for the unemployed, and miscellaneous pamphlets. (Note: See also Olson's papers in the Governors' Papers, State Archives.)

609. Olson, Robert A. (1894–1971). Papers, 1920–65. 2 folders.

Olson, a Duluth labor leader, was president of the Minnesota State Federation of Labor, 1938–53, and president of the Minnesota AFL-CIO, 1956–65. His papers include information on alleged Communist activity in the Federated Trades and Labor Assembly of Duluth and the Citizens Alliance of Duluth, speeches to various labor groups, and correspondence with conservative members of the Minnesota legislature.

610. On the Square Publishing Company, St. Paul. Records, 1917–18. 1 box.

The On the Square Publishing Co. was founded in order to publish an anti-NPL, anti-Socialist magazine during the 1918 elections. Only two issues were published due to a lack of advertisers and subscribers. The collection documents attempts to start up the paper and finance it from advertising revenue.

611. Orr, Charles Noah (1877–1949). Papers, 1896–1949. 2 boxes.

Orr served as a Republican in the Minnesota house, 1911–15, and in the Minnesota senate, 1915–49. His papers include information on the activities of the People's Lobby in the 1937 legislature and criticism of Governor Elmer Benson for encouraging the excesses of the People's Lobby.

612. Paull, Irene Levine (1908–81), collector. Papers Related to Progressive Politics and Labor Movements in Minnesota, 1934–69. 1 box. Restricted.

The collection contains correspondence, printed materials, reminiscences, and other papers. Included are folders about Chester Watson and the Workers Alliance, 1934–40; International Woodworkers of America, Local 12–29, 1944–59; mining and farm strikes, 1907 and 1947; and memorials for Henry Paull, 1947.

613. Pearson, Albert (1892?–1976). Papers, undated, 1968. 1 folder.

Pearson edited a Swedish-language Communist newspaper *Ny Tid,* 1929–36, in Chicago and New York. His papers include a 92-page untitled history in Swedish of the Scandinavian-American labor movement and its relationship to radical philosophies. Includes a translation by Michael Brook.

614. Pearson, Maney Maniece (1894–). Papers, 1940–60. (Duluth)

Pearson was active in the CIO Congress of Women's Auxiliaries. These papers include clippings, drafts of speeches, and reports on the Minnesota State CIO Council and its women's auxiliary.

615. Pedersen, Sigurd (1878–1969). Papers, 1911–39. 1 folder.

Pedersen was a teacher and edited the *Tyler Journal* in Tyler. The papers include letters written by Gunnar B. Bjornson, editor of the *Minneota Mascot,* which discuss socialism.

616. Pereault, Henry. Papers, 1889–1945. 2 folders.

Pereault was a member of the Cigarmakers Union of Duluth and president of the Minnesota Federation of Labor. The papers concern the general affairs of the Cigarmakers Union of Duluth and include a pamphlet, *Socialism and Trade Unionism* (1900), by Daniel Lynch.

617. Petersen, Hjalmar (1890–1968). Papers, 1907–68. 24 boxes.

Petersen served as lieutenant-governor under Floyd Olson, succeeding Olson as governor in 1936. He lost reelection in 1936 but served three terms as railroad and warehouse commissioner, 1937–43, 1955–66. His papers include correspondence and literature concerning the growing conflict within the Farmer-Labor Assn. over patronage, the possibility of the Democratic and F-L merger, and Communism. (Note: See also Petersen's papers in the Governors' Papers, State Archives.)

618. Petersen, Hjalmar (1890–1968). Papers, 1930–63. 3 boxes.

These papers supplement the collection above. They include general correspondence and information on Petersen's political career and document power shifts within the F-LP.

619. Peterson, Hjalmar Otto (1879–1957). Papers, 1930–45. 1 box.

Peterson was active in politics but held no offices. He worked for the NPL and the F-LP and published the *Washington County Post,* 1920–26. The collection includes articles by Peterson, correspondence, newspaper clippings, and scrapbooks. It documents dissention within the F-LP and NPL.

620. Power, Victor L. (?–1926). Papers, 1913–24. 3 boxes.

Power, a lawyer and Socialist, was mayor of Hibbing, 1913–22. He fostered many civic improvements by using a tax on the mining companies. He ran on the Republican ticket, unsuccessfully, for U.S. Congress in 1924. The collection consists of volumes that are a cross between diaries and scrapbooks, containing information on the 1916 IWW strike in Hibbing (Power supported the right to organize but opposed the IWW), prosecution of draft resisters, and the NPL's unsuccessful attempt to have Power run for state attorney general.

621. Preus, Jacob Aall Otteson (1883–1961), and Family. Papers, 1853–1946. 38 boxes.

Preus served as Republican governor of Minnesota, 1921–25. The collection reflects the threat that NPL activities in North Dakota and Minnesota posed to state governments and how the league's Socialist sympathies were used against it. Preus saw cooperative agriculture as an effective tool to lessen the influence of the NPL among farmers. The papers include printed materials on the IWW and Socialism, undated, 1853–1910, the IWW songbook, data on the International Joint Commission, the NPL and the strikes in the iron mines, and many anti-Socialist, anti-NPL pamphlets and speeches. (Note: See also Preus's papers in the Governors' Papers, State Archives.)

622. Quigley, Walter Eli (1890–1962). "Out Where the West Begins." 106 p.

Reminiscences of the development of the NPL through the 1932 F-L convention in Minnesota.

623. Reierson, Arthur O. (1905–65). Papers, undated, 1917, 1934–65. 6 boxes.

Reierson was a farmer, civic promoter, and political leader who built a strong faction of the F-LP in northwest Minnesota in the late 1930s. He organized and directed the Polk County DFL in the late 1940s and held a variety of DFL party positions, 1944–65. His papers include correspondence, speeches, and clippings concerning the F-LP.

624. Reitmeier, Edward H. "History of How the Farmers Union Came into Being." 1959. 4 p.

The collection includes information on the formation of the Farmers Union Oil Co., organized in 1933.

625. Robertson, Edwin Christian (1894–1965). Papers, 1931–32. 84 items.

Robertson was secretary of Minnesota's Liberty party, which supported F-L candidates. His papers include correspondence, platforms, and pamphlets concerning the Liberty party.

626. Rolvaag, Karl Fritjof (1913–90). Papers, 1939–84. 27 boxes. Restricted.

Rolvaag was DFL governor of Minnesota, 1963–67. His papers include materials on the F-LP, Floyd B. Olson, and other third parties. The inventory is not descriptive.

627. Romer, Sam (1913–65). Papers, 1948–64. 3 boxes.
Romer, a veteran of the Spanish Civil War, was a Socialist who became a labor journalist for the *Minneapolis Tribune*. He also wrote the book, *International Brotherhood of Teamsters* (1962). His papers include correspondence, notes, and clippings for the book.

628. Romer, Sam (1913–65). "Five Minutes That Changed the Face of Minneapolis," *Minneapolis Tribune*, July 19, 1964. 6 p.

Mounted newspaper clipping describing the Minneapolis truck drivers' strike of 1934.

629. Ross, Carl (1913–). Papers, 1935–76. 1 box. (IHRC)

Ross was secretary of the Labor Sports Union, 1930–34, secretary of the Young Communist League, 1935–37, editor of the *Työmies* Youth Section, 1930–34, and later *Clarity*, 1941–42, secretary of the Com-

munist party of the Minnesota-Dakotas district, and national secretary of American Youth for Democracy, 1943–45. Ross left the party in 1958. His papers include material on the history of the Finns in Minnesota.

630. Ross, Carl (1913–), and Family. Papers, 1946–58. 1 box.

Ross was secretary of the Young Communist League, 1935–37, and of the Minnesota Communist party, 1946–58. (See entry above.) The collection documents the activities of the Communist party in Minnesota.

631. Rowoldt, Charles (1883–). Papers, 1905, 1932, 1955–61. 4 folders.

Rowoldt immigrated to the U.S. from Germany but never became a citizen. He was secretary-treasurer of the Minneapolis chapter of the Workers Alliance in the 1930s. Deportation proceedings were brought against him several times. The collection contains correspondence and miscellaneous papers regarding these proceedings.

632. St. Anthony Turnverein, Minneapolis. Records, undated, 1868–1928, 1942. 7 boxes. In German, some English.

St. Anthony Turnverein was a German gymnastic society founded in 1857. The records include a 1906 appeal for donations to the IWW (in both German and English).

633. St. Paul Citizens' Association. Papers, 1903. 12 items.

This group was part of the Citizens' Industrial Association of America, which was founded in 1902 to curb the growing power of labor unions. The collection includes minutes of meetings, Sept. 29–Nov. 12, 1903, membership lists, and statements of principles.

634. St. Paul Plasterers and Cement Finishers Union, Local 20. Papers, 1917–32. 1 vol.

The papers consist of a minute book, which contains information on relations with other labor unions, political participation, the local's support of Tom Mooney, and membership in the Working People's NPL.

635. St. Paul Trades and Labor Assembly. Records, 1925–63. 4 boxes.

Minnesota's Socialist Workers party celebrated its 25th anniversary and commemorated the 1934 truck drivers' strike in this snapshot taken about 1951.

The records include minutes of meetings, attendance records, ledgers, and receipts.

636. St. Paul Trades and Labor Assembly. Papers, 1882–1937. 1 box.

The papers include minutes of meetings.

637. Series of Addresses on Labor Problems. 1932–33. Transcripts of 18 speeches, perhaps given over the radio, Mar.–June 1933. No authors or explanations are given. The point of view is generally probusiness. Subjects include racketeering in labor unions, the Farm Holiday Assn., legislation to enact a state income tax and unemployment insurance, economic conditions, Communism at home and in the USSR, labor union organizing drives, and wages paid for building the U.S. Post Office in Minneapolis.

638. Shipstead, Henrik (1881–1960). Papers, 1913–53. 33 boxes.

Shipstead was a U.S. Senator, 1923–47. He was elected as a Farmer-Laborite but became a Republican in 1940. The collection includes correspondence and other printed materials concerning agricultural conditions in Minnesota, the strength of the F-LP, Charles Lindbergh, Sr.'s, break with the NPL, the disorganization of the Republican party, dissension within the F-LP, and various other labor and political issues.

639. Smith, Edward E. (1861–1931). Papers, 1923–24. 4 folders.

Smith was a Spring Valley lawyer who served as a Republican in the Minnesota house, 1895–97, senate, 1899–1909, and as lieutenant-governor, 1910–11. He helped manage the campaigns of others. The papers focus on the filling of Senator Knute Nelson's position after his death and reveal the interest of many prominent politicians in the Republican nomination for the seat. The actual contest was among Republican Jacob Preus, Farmer-Laborite Magnus Johnson, and Democrat James Carley. Johnson won the nomination. Also included is information on an IWW pamphlet regarding Minneapolis employment offices.

640. Smith, Francis Monroe (1904–51). Papers, 1936–51. 3 boxes.

Smith was active in the Democratic party, 1928–44. He prepared the legal brief for the DFL merger in 1944. After 1948 he became active in the Progressive party and other liberal third-party organizations. His papers include materials concerning the conflict between the left- and right-wing factions of the DFL, 1947–48, the Progressive party, and prosecution of the Communist party under the Smith Act.

641. Snyder, Fred Beal (1859–1951). Papers, 1912–50. 14 boxes. (Uarch)

Snyder was a regent of the University of Minnesota, 1912–51. His papers include the complaints he received concerning radical and Communist activities on campus.

642. Socialist Labor Party of Minnesota, Minneapolis. Papers, 1908–64. 2 boxes.

The collection consists of pamphlets, speeches, clippings, and miscellaneous papers.

643. Socialist Party of America, Nashwauk. Papers, undated, 1906–13. 2 folders. In Finnish.

The collection consists of a financial ledger, 1906–13, and miscellaneous papers, including a copy of a 1912 Socialist party member's individual ballot.

644. Socialist Publishing Association. Papers, 1898. 4 p.

The association was an organ of the Socialist Labor party. Collection consists of its articles of incorporation, Mar. 15, 1898.

645. Socialist Workers Party, Minneapolis. Papers, undated, 1914–64. 10 boxes.

The collection consists of printed and mimeographed materials, campaign literature, newspaper clippings, pamphlets, and booklets. Most of it is from the national organization, and very little is specific to Minnesota. There are, however, materials on the 1941 sedition trial of the 18 leaders of the party, Motor Transport and Allied Workers Industrial Union, Local 544, the Carl Skoglund deportation case, 1949–51, the Albert Lea strike of the Wilson Co. by the United Packinghouse Workers in 1959, the DFL merger in Minnesota, and the 1948 elections, in which two Minnesotans—Farrell Dobbs and Grace Carlson—headed the national party ticket.

646. Socialist Workers Party, Minnesota. Records, 1941–81. 3 boxes. Restricted.

Although the records date mainly from the 1970s, there are miscellaneous newspaper clippings and printed fliers about political campaigns, 1944–57, and seven folders of mounted newspaper clippings on the 1941 trial of 18 party members for sedition under the Smith Act and the expulsion of the leadership of the Teamsters Union, Local 544.

647. Socialist Workers Party, Minnesota. Scrapbooks, 1941. 1 roll microfilm. Originals owned by Tom Kerry, New York, N.Y.

The collection contains information about the 1941 trial of party leaders and Teamsters Union, Local 544, prosecuted under the Smith Act for alleged subversive activities.

648. Sollie, Violet Johnson (1907–), and Allen N. Sollie (1898–1987). Papers, 1925–89. 4 boxes.

Violet Sollie was a F-L activist and the president of the Minneapolis branch of the League for Political Independence in the 1930s. She was a lifetime member of the Office and Professional Employees International Union. Allen Sollie was also a F-L activist in Minneapolis and served as Floyd Olson's Hennepin County campaign manager in 1934. Their papers include correspondence, printed memos, reports, articles, and clippings regarding their political activities.

649. Spielman, Jean E. (1882–1936). Papers, 1901–36. 16 rolls microfilm.

Spielman was a paid organizer for the IWW, 1912–13, and attempted to organize Minneapolis streetcar workers. He was expelled from the IWW in 1913, and in 1915 he became an AFL organizer. The papers focus on his work as a labor organizer and in the F-LP and include information on IWW activities, the Citizens Alliance, the Minneapolis Trades and Labor Assembly, the Minnesota Commission of Public Safety, and the destruction of IWW headquarters in Minneapolis, 1919. Also included are the Marshall Service Papers, 1918–23. Marshall Service, Inc., Kansas City, Mo., was a private detective agency used to bust unions especially in the flour milling industry, including IWW Local 460. These papers contain the notes for Spielman's book, *The Stool-Pigeon and the Open Shop Movement* (1923). Spielman sued Marshall Service to obtain their internal documents, which include letters accusing the IWW of being affiliated with a German spy system.

650. Stageberg, Susie Williamson (1877–1961). Papers, 1881–1961. 3 boxes.

Stageberg was active in the NPL and later became a founder of the F-LP. She was a F-L candidate for several state offices and Congress throughout the 1920s and 1930s and ran for lieutenant-governor on the 1950 Progressive party ticket. She wrote many articles for the *Organized Farmer*, the *Minnesota Leader*, the *Willmar Tribune*, the Norwegian-language *Minnesota Posten*, and other newspapers. Her papers consist of correspondence, articles, campaign literature, and newspaper clippings concerning the Farmer-

Labor Assn., the F-LP, the Women's Nonpartisan Club of Minnesota, and the struggle within the Hennepin County Farmer-Labor Assn. over allegations of Communist influence, 1936–40. Also included are typescripts of articles by Stageberg, undated, 1937–50.

651. Steel, James S., comp., 1963, 1976. Materials Relating to the Oliver Iron Mining Company, 1863–1972. 2 boxes.

The collection includes papers compiled for a possible book on the company. Includes information on ethnic groups on the iron range, Americanization, and labor problems, 1890s–1920.

652. Strikes and Lockouts. Miscellaneous Printed Items, 1916, 1937. 1 folder.

The collection contains selected items related to conditions on the Mesabi Iron Range leading to the miners' strike of 1916 and the strike against Twin Cities laundries by Dry Cleaners and Laundry Workers Union, Local 150, in 1937.

653. Strout, Irwin Charles (1893–1954). Papers, 1922–39. 12 boxes.

Strout was active in the North Dakota NPL and in F-L organizations throughout the 1920s. He became budget commissioner under Governor Olson and was at the center of the patronage issue. The papers include information about the F-LP's grass-roots struggle to gain power and Strout's role as an intermediary between the local and state F-L interests as the party gained control of state government. Also included is a file concerning the Farmer-Labor Education Bureau, 1934–35, which illuminates the party's political philosophy. Correspondents include Socialists and Communists.

654. Swanson, Samuel (1902–   ). Interview by Jack Spiese, 1967. 65 p. Photographic copy. Original in Pennsylvania State University, University Park, Penn.

Swanson was a labor leader in northern Minnesota. The interview describes life on the iron range, early attempts at unionization by the IWW and the Western Federation of Miners, information about Finns and other ethnic groups on the iron range, antiunion sentiment by the companies, and CIO activities after 1934. He stresses support among the workers for the Socialist, F-L, and the Communist parties and gives evidence of Communist activity in worker organizations.

655. Swenson, David Ferdinand (1876–1940). Papers, 1912–78. 3 boxes. (Uarch)

Swenson was a professor of philosophy at the University of Minnesota during the 1920s and 1930s. His papers include correspondence with Upton Sinclair concerning academic freedom, 1922–23, and in support of the formation of a Communist club at the university in 1937.

656. Teigan, Henry George (1881–1941). Papers, 1916–41. 51 boxes.

Teigan was secretary of the NPL, edited the *Minnesota Leader*, 1916–23, and later served as a Farmer-Laborite in the Minnesota senate, 1933–35, and house, 1937–39. The papers consist of correspondence, pamphlets, newspapers, and miscellaneous papers. The correspondence, 1916–41, is arranged chronologically in 33 boxes. The first four of them dating from Teigan's years as secretary of the NPL have been microfilmed as a supplement to the NPL collection.

657. Thomason, Otto Monroe (1874–1960), and Family. Papers, 1916–62. 15 items.

Thomason was an early leader of the NPL and edited the *Minnesota Leader*. He ran on the Socialist ticket for U.S. Congress in 1914 and was defeated by Republican Charles A. Lindbergh, Sr. The papers contain information on politics, economics, and peace.

658. Thompson, F. W. Letter, Dec. 1, 1929. 2 p. Photocopy. Original in Tamiment Institute Library, New York, N.Y.

Thompson was involved with the Work People's College in Duluth. He wrote this letter to Nathan Fine of the Rand School of Social Science about the college's curriculum, cooperative organization, enrollment, and finance.

659. Torma-Silvola Family. Papers, ca. 1901–79. 9 boxes. (IHRC)

Fred Torma immigrated to Nashwauk from Finland in 1906. He helped form the Elanto Cooperative, a grocery co-op, in 1908 and was a board member of the Central Cooperative Wholesale. Torma's son-in-law, Richard H. Silvola, served in the Minnesota house, 1945–53. Silvola was active in many Finnish-American organizations. The papers consist of scrapbooks, photographs, and organizational materials from various Finnish-American groups.

660. Townley, Arthur Channing (1880–1959). Biography File, 1956. 27 p.

Townley was a leader of the NPL in the 1910s and 1920s. The file includes several newspaper clippings about Townley's career.

661. Työmies Society, Superior. Records, 1903–70. 24 boxes, 1 roll microfilm. (IHRC)

The society began as a Finnish-American Socialist publishing company in 1903 and later became a Communist publishing house. Records include minutes of meetings, unpublished proletarian plays, sheet music, and correspondence received by Andrew Roine, head of the society, 1959–63. Also includes about 600 photographs.

662. Uebel, Ferdinand, and Family. Papers, 1882–1957. 1 box.

Uebel belonged to the Communist party, 1947–49. His papers include notices of meetings and lectures in Minneapolis and St. Paul, handbills, newspaper clippings, literature from the Henry A. Wallace campaign of 1948, assorted pamphlets opposing universal military training during World War I, and other miscellaneous political pieces.

663. United Garment Workers of America, Local 171, St. Paul. Papers, 1909–30. 2 vols.

The papers consist of two minute books that include information on relations with other unions, contributions to national labor causes, such as the campaign to free Tom Mooney, and aid to Russian peasants.

664. United States. Eighth District Court of Appeals. *Dunne vs. United States, 1943.* Abstract of the Record, Briefs, and Opinion. (Conspiracy Trials in America, no. 13). 1 roll microfilm. Published by Michael Glazier, Inc.

The item consists of the appeal of the convictions of 18 members of the Socialist Workers party who had been among the leaders of Minneapolis Teamsters' Local 544, tried in 1941 for sedition under the Smith Act. The appeal was denied.

665. University of Minnesota. Office of the Dean of Students. Papers, 1904–45. 92 boxes. (Uarch)

Papers include a file on the Seekers, a radical student club, 1919–20, to whose meetings the dean sent observers. The observers' reports describe the club's activities and its discussions of feminism, academic freedom, and the Committee of 48.

666. University of Minnesota. President's Office. Papers, 1911–45, 1946–60. 135 boxes. (Uarch)

Papers include files on academic freedom, speaker policy, Communism in the McCarthy era, and radicalism in 1935.

667. Valesh, Eva MacDonald. Reminiscences, 1952, 1957. 69 p., 3 p. 1 roll microfilm. Originals in Columbia University, New York, N.Y.

Valesh, a newspaper reporter and lecturer, was an organizer for the Minnesota Farmers' Alliance in the 1890s. She later moved to the East Coast, where she continued to write and organize for the AFL. The three-page manuscript is a memoir by Valesh's sister, Blanche MacDonald. The 69-page transcript contains excerpts from the microfilmed interview of Valesh by Wendell H. Link, 1952.

668. Videen, Clayton A. (1911–   ). Research notes, 1887–1920. 1 box. Restricted.

The collection includes copies of newspapers and magazine articles selected and annotated by Videen as part of a project to compile a labor history, 1889–1920, for the WPA Worker Education Program in Duluth. Topics include strike activities in Duluth, 1887, 1920, on the Mesabi and Cuyuna iron ranges, 1907, 1916, and by the Timber Workers Union in Cloquet, 1920. Also covered are the Western Federation of Miners in 1907, public opinion and investigatory commissions, the Oliver Iron Mining Co., the role of ethnic minorities in strikes, and the activities of the Timber Workers Union in the 1910 strike.

669. Volstead, Andrew John (1860–1947), and Family. Papers, 1868–1955. 7 boxes.

Volstead was a Republican in the U.S. House, 1903–23. He was the author of the 1919 prohibition amendment. His papers include a 1919 volume entitled "Collective Bargaining for Farmers" and a 1920 volume, "Sedition." Both volumes are proceedings of congressional hearings.

670. Wagner, Albert G. Papers, 1908–19. 1 box.

Wagner was interested in the IWW and anarchism and wrote many sympathetic articles about them. His papers contain these articles and his personal correspondence about politics and economics.

671. Waite, Edward Foote (1860–1958), and Family. Papers, 1764–1958. 5 items.

Waite served as judge of the Fourth Judicial District of Minnesota, 1911–41, and was interested in social welfare, civil rights, and civil liberties. The papers consist of his correspondence and political papers and contain information on a variety of social welfare topics, including congressional legislation requiring U.S. Communist organizations to register.

672. Wattson, Marshman S. (1912–62). Papers Relating to Pierce Butler's Appointment to the United States Supreme Court, 1917–22. 1 box.

Transcripts of letters and U.S. Senate hearings include unfavorable testimony about Butler's term as a University of Minnesota regent when Professor Stanley I. Rypins was dismissed due to his involvement in the Committee of 48 and other progressive causes.

673. Wefald, Knud (1869–1936). Papers, 1817–1987. 52 boxes.

Wefald, a farmer from Hawley, served in the Minnesota legislature, 1913–16, in the U.S. Congress, 1923–27, and in various state administrative positions, including railroad and warehouse commissioner, 1933–36. The collection consists of correspondence, legislation, speeches, articles, reports, clippings, minutes, and other materials relating to Floyd B. Olson, Communists in the F-LP, NPL support of Wefald, various political campaigns, the NPL's future, Wefald's role in the F-LP, the Committee of 48, the Socialist party, Magnus Johnson, the People's Reconstruction League, the Public Ownership League, the 1927 F-LP convention in St. Paul, the Minneapolis truck drivers' strike in 1934, and a scrapbook containing political clippings, 1922–28.

674. Wefald, Magnus (1900–91), and Family. Papers, 1877–1988. 90 boxes. Restricted.

Magnus Wefald was Minnesota senator, 1947–59. The collection includes legal files, correspondence, speeches, files of Interim Commissions, personal papers, and newspaper clippings. Supplements the Knud Wefald Papers.

675. Wier, Roy William (1888–1963). Papers, undated, 1920–63. 6 boxes.

Wier was a F-L representative in the Minnesota house, 1933–39, and a DFL congressman, 1949–61. His papers include materials on the House Un-American Activities Committee, 1948–60.

676. Wiita, John (1888–   ). Papers, 1975–84. 1 box. (IHRC)

Wiita immigrated to Superior from Finland in 1905. He worked as a longshoreman and railroad car repairman and was active in the Superior chapter of the Finnish Socialist Federation. He was also associated with the Work People's College in Duluth. Wiita's papers include correspondence with historian Michael Karni, an autobiography, short sketches of labor history, and biographies of Finnish Americans.

677. Williams, Howard Yolen (1889–1973). Papers, 1924–70. 48 boxes.

Williams, a pastor at People's Church in St. Paul, 1919–29, was active in F-L politics. His papers consist of correspondence and other printed materials concerning his activities in third-party organizations, such as the League for Independent Political Action, 1929–36, the Farmer-Labor Political Federation, 1933–35, the American Commonwealth Political Federation, 1935–37, the Union for Democratic Action, 1941–45, the Independent Voters of Illinois, 1945–46, and the American League for a Free Palestine, 1946–47. Included in the inventory is a list of officers of various organizations and information on the conflict within these groups and their problems in cooperating with the Socialist and Communist parties.

678. Work People's College, Duluth. Records, 1904–62. 6 boxes, 1 roll microfilm. In Finnish, some English. (IHRC)

The college was founded in 1903 as the Finnish People's College and Theological Seminary in Minneapolis. Its purpose was to train clergy and educate Finnish Americans in general. The school was moved to the Duluth suburb of Smithville, where more Finnish immigrants had settled. By 1908 Finnish Socialists had gained control of the school and renamed it the Work People's College (Työväen-Opisto). The school was affiliated with the Finnish Socialist Federation until the schism in 1914, after which it became a labor school for the IWW. It ceased holding classes in 1940. Records of the college contain correspondence, financial records, student club minutes, student rosters, and proletarian plays.

679. Workers' Publishing Company, Duluth. Records, ca. 1915–75. 6 boxes. In Finnish. (IHRC)

The company was founded in 1914 as the Socialist Publishing Co. by Finnish industrial unionists. It published a daily newspaper, *Socialisti.* In 1916 the paper was renamed *Teollisuustyöläinen* (The Industrial Worker). A lawsuit was brought against the paper and in 1917 it reappeared as *Industrialisti,* published by the newly formed Workers' Socialist Publishing Co. The Workers' Socialist Publishing Co. was closely allied to the Work People's College in Duluth. In 1954 the company changed its name to the Workers' Publishing Co. In 1975 *Industrialisti,* one of the last foreign-language IWW newspapers in the U.S., ceased publication. Records include correspondence, financial statements, and office files.

680. Workers' Socialist Publishing Company, Duluth. Papers, undated, 1910–57. 3 boxes. In Finnish.

The company was associated with the IWW and published *Industrialisti.* Papers consist of correspondence (in Finnish) and other miscellaneous papers.

681. Young, Douglas S. Papers, 1943–70. 3 boxes.

Young was the administrative assistant to Republican Governor Harold LeVander, 1969–70. His papers include Communist political literature and mailings from the 1940s and 1950s.

682. Young Pioneers of Minneapolis. Speech. 1929. 6 p.

The Young Pioneers was the Communist party's children's group. It began around 1929 and sponsored summer camps, plays, and speeches until about 1938. This speech, dated Nov. 1929 and written for the 12th anniversary of the Russian Revolution, focused on advances in child care and education in the Soviet Union as compared with the U.S. The identity of the writer is unknown.

683. Youngdahl, Luther Wallace (1896–1978). Papers, undated, 1923–67. 7 boxes.

Youngdahl was a Minnesota supreme court judge who served as Republican governor, 1947–51. He served on the U.S. District Court for Washington, D.C., 1951–78. His papers include correspondence and related papers on the Owen Lattimore case. Lattimore had been accused of disloyalty in 1952 for his involvement with the Institute of Pacific Relations and the magazine, *Amerasia,* both alleged to have supported Chinese Communists' overthrow of Chiang Kai-shek. Youngdahl dismissed charges against Lattimore, and files show letters of support and nonsupport, 1953–56. (Note: See also Youngdahl's papers in the Governors' Papers, State Archives.)

Sound and Visual Collection

The Minnesota Historical Society's Sound and Visual Collection includes videorecordings, sound recordings, films, posters, and photographs. The items listed below are selected from the collections of the Minnesota Historical Society.

VIDEORECORDINGS, SOUND RECORDINGS, AND FILMS

These items are accessible through the computerized catalog. In addition to the materials described here, there are many untitled recordings of radio call-in programs and political speeches, plus untitled filmed footage of political figures, demonstrations, and related subject matter; although not cataloged, these untitled items are listed by subject in finding aids for these collections.

684. *Children of Labor: A Finnish-American History* [videorecording]. Minneapolis: River City Video, 1984. 1 videocassette, 40 min.

A video about the social and political lives of Finnish immigrants who settled in northern Minnesota. Produced by the Finnish-American Bicentennial Committee and the Minnesota Humanities Commission.

685. *A Common Man's Courage* [videorecording]. Minneapolis: University Community Video, 1978. Written and produced by Jim Mulligan and John De Graaf. 1 videocassette, 44 min.

The story of John T. Bernard, Minnesota congressman who cast the only vote against the embargo on shipping arms to Spain in 1937.

686. "The Communist Russian New Deal Game to Bankrupt the U.S.A." [sound recording] by A. C. Townley. N.p.: A. C. Townley, 1956. 1 sound disc, 45 min.

687. *Labor's Turning Point: The Minneapolis Truck Strikes of 1934: A Rank and File Story* [videorecording]. St. Paul:

John De Graaf, Twin Cities Public Television, 1981. 1 videocassette, 44 min.

688. [Newsreels], Paramount, 1934–49. 2 reels, 15 min., 30 min.

This collection of newsreels from the 1930s includes: 1) "Farmers Threaten Strike," five Midwest governors call on president, Governor Olson speaks, calling for fixed prices on agricultural goods (1935?); 2) "Political Pot Comes to a Boil," former President Hoover speaks against federal programs, Floyd B. Olson calls for a national third party in 1936, 3) "Farmer-Labor Group Enters as Third Party," F-L convention, 1936; 4) "A City Ruled by Troops," Minneapolis truckers' strike, National Guard marching in city, 1934; 5) "Strike Outbreak Fatal," scenes of violence and conflict between strikers and deputies, Minneapolis truckers' strike, 1934; 6) "Move for Labor Peace," fighting and shooting between strikers and deputies, Minneapolis truckers' strike, 1934; 7) "Security for Americans," unemployment compensation, Secretary of Labor Frances Perkins, and Floyd B. Olson; 8) "Meat Strike, St. Paul, 1948," scenes at stockyards with strikers and National Guard. (Note: Individual films are not on the computerized catalog.)

689. *People, Pride and Politics: Building the North Star Country* [sound recording]. [Minneapolis]: Pandora Productions, [1979?].

Based on materials collected by Meridel Le Sueur. Features firsthand accounts of early farm organizing and unemployed organizing in the 1930s. Includes Madge Hawkins and Clarence Sharp.

690. "Raspberry Festival" [motion picture]. 1941, 1944. 6 min.

Filmed footage shows Socialist Workers party members at their 1941 and 1944 annual Raspberry Festivals at the home of Howard Carlson, 6500 15th Avenue South, Richfield. Party members shown include

A group of Socialists picnicked with their families at Arcola in 1916, displaying banners that advertised their town, Stillwater, and political affiliation, "Socialism Will Abolish Wage Slavery." Photographer John Runk put himself into the photo; he stands fifth from the left.

Oscar Coover, Sr., Carl Skoglund, Vincent Dunne, Grace Carlson, Jake Cooper, Harry DeBoer, Clarence Hamel, Goldie Cooper, Winifred Chelstrom, Oscar Schonfeld, and Howard Carlson.

691. *Roots of Reform: A Study of the Political History of the Upper Midwest with Special Emphasis on the Populist Movement* [videorecording]. Written and produced by James Dooley, [1989]. 3 videocassettes, 60 min. each.
   Broadcast by public television station KTCA, St. Paul, May 1970.

692. [Socialist Workers Party Activities, motion picture, 1957]. 1 reel, 13 min.
   Filmed footage shows members at a 1957 St. Patrick's Day celebration at the party offices at 322 Hennepin Avenue, Minneapolis. Also includes footage of members at the party camp in Los Angeles, Calif.

693. [Socialist Workers Party Activities, motion picture, 1956–57]. 1 reel, 25 min.
   Filmed footage features a welcome home celebration for Vincent R. Dunne and housewarming for new party headquarters at 322 Hennepin Avenue, Minneapolis, Jan. 19, 1957; a rummage sale on May 12, 1956, at 2700 Riverside Avenue, Minneapolis; a May 19, 1956, songfest with the Minnesota Mili-

tant Chorus; a 1956 Memorial Day picnic at Parker's Point; a speech by Myra T. Weiss on June 8, 1956; the 1956 Annual Strawberry Festival at Bill and Jean Brust's house, 715 South Lexington, St. Paul; a campaign dinner for Farrell Dobbs on Oct. 6, 1956; and other activities.

PHOTOGRAPHS AND POSTERS

Photographs in the Sound and Visual Collection are organized by subject and place. They are housed in folders that are arranged by call number according to a subject classification system developed at the Minnesota Historical Society as an expansion of the Library of Congress headings. Researchers can look up subject headings of interest in the subject-and-place card catalog, find a call number, and call for photos using photo call slips. The collection also has a portrait catalog that lists photos of specific people. Individual photos are not currently accessible through the computerized catalog, but photo albums and collections or groups of photos can be located through the computerized catalog.

The size of the photo collection and the ambiguous nature of what actually relates to "radicalism" prevent a listing of everything that is available. Some particularly fruitful subject headings, however, are listed below.

Labor. Disputes. Strikes and lockouts, which is further divided by industry, for photos of strikes, demonstrations, riots, resulting property damage, and relief efforts. Photos of the Minneapolis truckers' strike of 1934, for instance, include the women's auxiliary soup kitchen, which fed the teamsters, and the July 1934 funeral of striker Henry Ness, who was killed while picketing, as well as pictures of the violent clashes between strikers and deputies.

Labor. Laboring classes, for photos of workers, working conditions, and employee facilities.

Labor. Organizations, divided further by activities and institutions, for photos of labor activists, demonstrations, and meetings.

Politics and Government, further divided by *Organized Political Parties, Political campaigns,* and *Political Action Groups,* for photos of Socialists, Communists, Farmer-Laborites, their demonstrations, political campaigns, and other activities.

Industry, Unemployment, and *Transportation,* and the subdivisions of these three categories, are photos of working and living conditions, equipment, and workers that may be helpful in understanding labor disputes and subsequent negotiations.

Photographs are also available within the State Archives and Manuscripts Collections. There are four three-ring binders of photographs in the Manuscripts Collections, but these are not comprehensive, and researchers are encouraged to search beyond these binders. Photos in these collections are not organized separately but found interfiled in certain papers and records. The listings in the Archival and Manuscript Collections section (see Chapter 4) of this bibliography provide a good starting place for tracking down photos in these collections.

Posters in the Audio-Visual Collection are organized, like the photographs, according to subject. There is a three-ring binder containing slides of most of the posters available. Posters of interest include: poster to get the Communists out of the F-LP; advertisement for speeches by Robert Minor (of the Communist party), Ella Winter (Mrs. Lincoln Steffens), and Mayor Thomas Van Lear; various calls to strike; antiwar posters concerning both World War I and World War II; anti-New Deal posters; and various Communist party and Socialist posters. Posters are also included in the pamphlets and ephemera collections.

Artifacts at the Minnesota Historical Society

Listed below are selected items relating to Minnesota radicalism in the Museum Collection of the Minnesota Historical Society. The listing is a sampling only. For more information, consult the loan research coordinator of the Museum Collection.

694. Pine plank with "A.N.I.U. MEMBERS OF THE I.W.W./ A. KOSKE," carved into it. Ca. 1907–17.

The A.N.I.U. refers possibly to the Agricultural National Industrial Union, a subdivision of the IWW. The plank was found in an abandoned logging camp at Bear's Head Lake, St. Louis County. Its date is uncertain, but it was probably carved sometime between 1907 and 1917, the peak years of the IWW in Minnesota. While the IWW was outlawed in 1917, it seems unlikely that this would have prevented any of its members from carving into a board a declaration of their membership in the outlawed organization.

695. Nonpartisan League pennant: "FARMER/WE'LL STICK/LABOR" in red and white paint inside a bull's-eye target. Triangular navy cotton cloth pennant. 1915.

696. Nonpartisan League banner: "Lindbergh for Governor—We'll Stick, We'll Win." Painted white cloth. 1918.

The society has two of these.

697. Socialist party certificate: "This certifies that J. Kittelson by supporting the Socialist Party during the world crisis of 1918 kept faith with International Socialism and the cause of the workers." Paper. Ca. 1919–20.

698. Nonpartisan League banner: "FARMER/LABOR/ WE'LL STICK." Triangular blue cotton cloth, 29 inches long. Ca. 1920s.

Artifacts in the MHS collections related to radical activities include buttons, banners, and billy clubs. Pictured here are buttons promoting the Nonpartisan League, the Workers Alliance, Local 574 of the Minneapolis General Drivers and Helpers Union, which began the famous 1934 teamsters' strike in that city, and a banner advertising One Big Union, a slogan of the Industrial Workers of the World.

699. IWW banner: "ONE BIG UNION." Triangular red felt, 2 feet long. Ca. 1920s.

700. Oak "billy club" issued to supervisors and strike breakers by the Twin City Rapid Transit Co. during a bitter strike in the 1920s. Ca. 1920s.

James C. Thomblison, a long-time employee of the company and an active member of the Amalgamated Street Railway Union gave the club to Douglas Alan Bruce during a 1972 interview (see no. 354).

701. Working People's Non-Partisan Political League of Minnesota membership card. Signed by Secretary-Treasurer Thomas Van Lear. Ca. 1921–22.

Includes statement of purpose.

702. Working People's Non-Partisan Political League of Minnesota membership card. Stamp booklet for 1921–22.

703. Two insignia from the Abraham Lincoln Brigade uniform of Clarence Forester who served in the Lincoln Brigade of the Spanish Republic Army. 1937–38. (see no. 316).

704. BUTTONS:

Thomas Meighen for Governor, 1902, People's Party

Nonpartisan League buttons: Farmer/Labor/ We'll Stick

Farmer-Labor buttons

Minneapolis General Drivers and Helpers Union, Local 574, 1934

Vote IUE–CIO

Gasoline and Oil Drivers, Bulk Plant Employees, and Filling Station Operators, Local 975, 1939

Workers Alliance, 1939

Wallace for President, 1948, Progressive Party

Periodicals

Most of the periodicals listed below are in the Minnesota Historical Society Research Center. Those located at the Immigration History Research Center (IHRC) or the University of Minnesota Archives (Uarch) are so identified. Each entry includes the periodical's title, place of publication, publisher, duration, frequency of publication (if known), and repository holdings. Periodicals at the Minnesota Historical Society Research Center are accessible through the computerized catalog.

705. *Action.* Minneapolis: Communist Party, Minnesota-Dakotas District, 1946–?. Frequency unknown.
MHS holdings: Oct. 9, 1946–Apr. 1948

706. *Ahjo* (The Forge). Duluth: Työväen-Opisto [Work People's College], 1915–21. Quarterly. In Finnish. (IHRC)
The publication called itself a "socialist-scientific-literary" periodical. It was closely associated with the IWW.
IHRC holdings: 1 (1916)–6 (1921)

707. *America First.* St. Paul: Tom Parker Junkin, 1919(?)–(?). Monthly.
Antiradical magazine. Edited by Tom Parker Junkin.
MHS holdings: Apr.–Oct. 1919

708. *Americanism Bulletin.* Faribault: W. D. Herrstrom, 1950(?)–(?). Monthly.
MHS holdings: no. 17 (Sept. 1951), no. 20 (Dec. 1951)–no. 24 (Apr. 1952)

709. *Appeal to Reason.* Minneapolis: Tom Paine Branch of the Communist Party, 1940–(?). Irregular.
MHS holdings: 1:1–7 (Aug. 1940–May 8, 1941)

710. *Campus Challenge.* Minneapolis: Minnesota Young Communist League, 1939–40. Monthly. (Uarch)
Uarch holdings: 1 (1939–40)

711. *CIO Industrial Unionist.* Minneapolis: Hennepin County Industrial Council of the CIO, 1937–(?). Frequency unknown.
MHS holdings: 1:1 (Dec. 1, 1937). (Note: Microfilmed on roll called "Miscellaneous Minneapolis Newspapers")

712. *Citizens Alliance Bulletin.* Minneapolis: Citizens Alliance, 1917–32(?). Monthly.
MHS holdings: 1:8 (Aug. 1917)–16:5 (May 1932)

713. *Co-operative Pyramid Builder.* Superior: Central Co-op Exchange, 1926–(?). Frequency varies. (IHRC)
Called *Co-operative Builder* after 1931. This publication featured political articles, short stories, poems, and sections on health and agriculture and was central to Finnish activism in the cooperative movement. Originally the periodical carried a militant socialist line, which gradually disappeared from its pages through the 1930s. Editors included George Halonen, Oscar Cooley, and Erick Kendall.
IHRC holdings: 1932–46, 1953–76 (Note: Some years missing, holdings incomplete)

714. *Folke-Kalender 1917.* Skandinavisk Socialist Forbund. Chicago: Scandinavian Workers Publishing Society, 1917–(?). Annual. In Norwegian.
Yearbook combines articles, statistics, and poetry with reports and photos from Scandinavian Socialist Alliance branches in Illinois, Minnesota (Duluth, St. Paul, Minneapolis), Wisconsin, Washington, and several eastern states. Includes ads from businesses in Illinois and Duluth.
MHS holdings: no. 1 (1917)

715. *Gopher Communist.* Minneapolis: University of Minnesota Branch of the Young Communist League, 1937. Frequency unknown. (Uarch)
Uarch holdings: Nov. 11, 1937

716. *Industrialistin Joulu* (Industrialist Christmas).

An often-published cartoon that appeared in the August 19, 1916, issue of Solidarity *depicts the Steel Trust and other puny opponents as the only impediment to the achievement of emancipation by Mesabi miners working with the Industrial Workers of the World.*

Duluth: Workers Socialist Pub. Co., 1917–60. Annual. In Finnish. (IHRC)

> Annual Christmas publication. Continued *Sosialistin Joulu*.
> IHRC holdings: 1917–28, 1946–60

717. *Kansan Huumori* (Popular Humor). New York: Communist Finnish Federation, Inc., and Superior: Työmies Pub. Co., 1936–38. Semimonthly. In Finnish, some English.

> Published by the Communist Finnish Federation in New York and printed by the Työmies Press in Superior. Editors included K. A. Suvanto, Kalle Rissanen, and Toivo Korpela. Periodical contained comics, jokes, stories, and poems about social and political issues. Succeeded *Punikki*. Ceased in 1938.
> MHS and IHRC holdings: 26:5 (Mar. 1, 1936)–28:15 (Aug. 1, 1938)

718. *Labor Digest*. Minneapolis: Union Pub. Co., 1908–23. Monthly, 1908–19, irregular, 1920–23.

> A. E. Stevens was editor.
> MHS holdings: 1:1 (Jan. 1908)–15:? (Dec. 1923)

719. *Lapa Tossu* (Shoepack). Hancock, Mich.: Työmies Pub. Co., 1911–14; Superior: Työmies Pub. Co., 1914–21. Semimonthly. In Finnish. (MHS and IHRC)

> This popular periodical moved from Hancock to Superior in 1914 with its publishing company, Työmies. Its editors included K. A. Suvanto, Jukka

Salminen, and J. L. Kyyrö. The paper originally followed the Socialist line, but gradually turned Communist, after the Socialist-Communist split in the late 1910s. The paper contained jokes, stories, sketches, and cartoons. Succeeded in 1921 by *Punikki*.
> IHRC holdings: 1 (1911)–6 (1916), 8 (1918), Apr. 10 (1920)
> MHS holdings: 7:1 (Jan. 1, 1917)–11:8 (Apr. 15, 1921)

720. *Militant Socialist*. Minneapolis: Socialist Party of Minnesota, 1936. Frequency unknown.

> MHS holdings: July 1936

721. *Minneapolis Teacher: Special Strike Bulletin*. Minneapolis, 1948. Daily.

> Bulletin of the Minneapolis teachers' strike, 1948. Produced by E. R. Newstrand and Sophie Albinson, members of the strike staff.
> MHS holdings: no. 1–18 (Feb. 29–Mar. 22, 1948)

722. *Minnesota Artist*. Minneapolis: Minnesota Artists' Union, 1938–39. Frequency irregular.

> Continues *Minnesota Artists Union Bulletin*. Called *Bulletin (United American Artists of Minnesota)* after 1940.
> MHS holdings: Nov. 1938–Oct. 1939, Apr. 1, 1940, Oct. 29, 1941

723. *Minnesota Artists Union Bulletin*. Minneapolis: Minnesota Artists' Union, 1937–38. Frequency irregular.

Continued in 1938 by *Minnesota Artist*.
MHS holdings: Oct. 15, 1937–Oct. 8, 1938

724. *Minnesota Communist*. Minneapolis: State Organization Education Committee, Communist Party, 1937–(?). Frequency unknown.
MHS holdings: 1:1 (Jan. 1937)

725. *Minnesota Facts*. Minneapolis: Minnesota Communist Party, 1939–(?). Monthly.
MHS holdings: 1:1–8 (May–Dec. 1939)

726. *Minnesota Federationist*. St. Paul: Minnesota State Federation of Labor, 1927–56. Monthly and semimonthly.
Continued by the AFL-CIO after 1956.
MHS holdings: 1:1 (Sept. 15, 1927)–29:6 (May 15, 1956)

727. *On the Square: A Magazine for the Farm and Home*. St. Paul: On the Square Pub. Co., 1918. Monthly.
A. M. Van Hosen, editor. "In each issue . . . we are going to fight . . . the socialism of the National Nonpartisan League."
MHS holdings: 1:1–2 (May–June 1918)

728. *The Patriot*. Minneapolis: All American Society, 1923. Frequency unknown.
MHS holdings: 1:1 (Sept. 1923)

729. *Punanen Soihtu* (Red Torch). Duluth: Workers Socialist Pub. Co., 1915–41. Annual. In Finnish. (IHRC)
Closely connected to *Industrialisti* and the IWW.
IHRC holdings: 1916–27, 1938–41

730. *Punikki* (The Red). Superior: Työmies Pub. Co., 1921–31; New York: Communist Finnish Federation, Inc., 1931–36. Semimonthly. In Finnish. (MHS and IHRC)
Succeeded *Lapa Tossu*. K. A. Suvanto edited the periodical, and writers included Moses Hahl, Kalle Rissanen, and Mikael Rutanen. This popular periodical contained comics, "philosophical reviews," short stories, and jokes on political and social issues. After 1931 it was published by the communist Finnish Workers Federation. Succeeded by *Kansan Huumori* in 1936.
MHS and IHRC holdings: 11:9 (May 1, 1921)–26:4 (Feb. 15, 1936)

731. *Rebel Poet*. Holt, Minn.: B. C. Hagglund, 1931–32. Monthly.

Official organ of the Rebel Poets, an association of Communist writers. Editors included B. C. Hagglund and Jack Conroy. Continued in 1933 by *The Anvil* in New York.
MHS holdings: 1:1 (Jan. 1931)–1:17 (Oct. 1932)

732. *Sosialistin Joulu* (Socialist Christmas). Duluth: Workers Socialist Pub. Co., 1914–16. Annual. In Finnish. (IHRC)
Annual Christmas publication. Continued in 1917 by *Industrialistin Joulu*.
IHRC holdings: 1914–16

733. *Student Unity*. Minneapolis: University of Minnesota Unit of the Young Communist League, 1935. Frequency unknown. (Uarch)
Uarch holdings: 1:1 (Dec. 2, 1935)

734. *Telling Facts*. St. Paul: Facts Pub. Co., 1938–40. Monthly.
Catholic anti-Communist magazine.
MHS holdings: 1:1 (Nov. 1938)–2:4 (Feb. 1940)

735. *Tie Vapauteen* (Road to Freedom). New York: The IWW-Finns of the East, 1919–29; Duluth: Workers Socialist Pub. Co., 1929–37. Monthly. In Finnish, some English. (IHRC)
The periodical called itself an "industrialist-scientific-literary monthly," carried no advertising, and included a section in English. Its place of publication and editorship varied yearly, although its ties to the IWW line remained steady. Editors included Tobias Kekkonen, Tiitus Kataja, Jack Ujanen, and Iivari Vapaa. Frequent contributors included Kalle Rissanen, Yrjö Sirola, and William Tanner.
IHRC holdings: 1 (1919)–19 (1937)

736. *Työläisten Taskukalentari* (Workingman's Pocket Calendar). Duluth: Workers Socialist Pub. Co., 1910–52(?). Annual. In Finnish. (IHRC)
IHRC holdings: 1924–25, 1927, 1932, 1934–35, 1938, 1946–48, 1950, 1952

737. *Työmiehen Joulu* (Workingman's Christmas). Hancock, Mich., Superior: Amerikan Suomalaisten Sosialististen Kuustannusliikke, 1904–29. Annual. In Finnish. (MHS and IHRC)
MHS holdings: no. 9 (1911)–no. 20 (1922) (Note: Some issues missing)
IHRC holdings: no. 5 (1907)–no. 12 (1914), 1916–29

738. *Uuden Ajan Joulu* (Christmas of the New Era). Duluth: Workers Socialist Pub. Co., 1937–45. Annual. (IHRC)

    IHRC holdings: 1937–45

739. *Voice of the Rondo District*. St. Paul: Rondo Unit of the Communist Party, 1939–40(?). Frequency unknown.

    MHS holdings: May 1939–Sept. 1940

740. *Warrior News*. Minneapolis: Northwest Warriors Committee on Americanization, 1920–(?).

    Anti-Communist paper.

MHS holdings: 1:1 (Jan. 5, 1920). (Note: Microfilmed on roll called "Miscellaneous Minneapolis Newspapers")

741. *Work People's College Bulletin*. [Duluth]: Students of the College, 1924–(?).

    MHS holdings: 1:4 (Jan. 15, 1924)

742. *WPA and Relief News*. Minneapolis: Workers Alliance of America, Hennepin County Committee, 1936–(?).

    MHS holdings: 1:1 (Sept. 14, 1936)

Books, Unpublished Papers, and Articles

Most of the publications and papers listed below were selected from the collections of the Minnesota Historical Society. Those located at the Immigration History Research Center (IHRC) or the University of Minnesota Archives (Uarch) are so identified. The list is not exhaustive, but a sampling. Items at the Minnesota Historical Society Research Center are accessible through the computerized catalog.

BOOKS

743. Browder, Earl. *Mita on Sosialifascismi, sen Historiiallinen j Teoreetinen Tausta.* Superior: Työmies Society, 1934. 61 p. In Finnish. (IHRC)

744. Browder, Earl. *Victory—and After.* New York: International Publishers, 1942. 256 p. Translated by Leo Mattson as *Voitto—Ja Sen Jälkeen.* Superior: Työmies Society, 1943. In Finnish. (IHRC)

745. Bullock, Edna Dean, comp. *Selected Articles on Trade Unions.* Minneapolis: H. W. Wilson Co., 1913. 262 p.

746. Casey, Larry, ed. *Labor and Politics: A Manual of Readings.* Minneapolis: Labor Education Service, Industrial Relations Center, University of Minnesota, 1986. 106 p.

747. Chrislock, Carl H. *Watchdog of Loyalty: The Minnesota Commission of Public Safety During World War I.* St. Paul: Minnesota Historical Society Press, 1991. 387 p.

748. Critchlow, Donald T., ed. *Socialism in the Heartland: The Midwestern Experiences, 1900–25.* Notre Dame: University of Notre Dame Press, 1986. 221 p.
Includes "Hothouse Socialism, Minneapolis, 1910–1925," by David Paul Nord, p. 133–166. Includes bibliographies and index.

749. Dobbs, Farrell. *Teamster Bureaucracy.* New York: Monad Press, 1977. 304 p.

750. Dobbs, Farrell. *Teamster Politics.* New York: Monad Press, 1975. 256 p.

751. Dobbs, Farrell. *Teamster Power.* New York: Monad Press, 1973. 255 p.

752. Dobbs, Farrell. *Teamster Rebellion.* New York: Monad Press, 1972. 190 p.

753. Farmer-Labor Party (Minnesota). *Speakers Manual: Material for Speakers in Behalf of Governor Olson.* N.p., n.d. 64 p.
This manual appeared in several different editions.

754. Gieske, Millard L. *Minnesota Farmer-Laborism: The Third Party Alternative.* Minneapolis: University of Minnesota Press, 1979. 389 p.

755. Halme, Kaarlo. *Sirpin ja Vasaran Maasta, Kertomuksia* (Stories from the Land of the Hammer and Sickle). Superior: Amerikan Suomalainen Sosialistinen Kustannusliike, 1928. 106 p. In Finnish. (IHRC)

756. Halonen, A. *Suomen Luokkasota, Historiaa ja Muistelmia* (The Finnish Class War). Superior: Amerikan Suomalainen Sosialistinen Kustannusliike, 1928. 525 p. In Finnish. (IHRC)
A history of the Finnish civil war of 1917–18. The "reds" were defeated in Finland, and many of them came to the U.S., where the conflicts from the Old Country continued.

757. Harrington, Jeremiah C. *Catholicism, Capitalism, or Communism.* St. Paul: E. M. Lohmann Co., 1926. 445 p.

758. Haynes, John Earl. *Dubious Alliance: The Making*

of Minnesota's DFL Party. Minneapolis: University of Minnesota Press, 1984. 264 p.

759. Hoerder, Dirk, ed. *The Immigrant Labor Press in North America, 1840s–1970s: An Annotated Bibliography.* 3 vols. New York: Greenwood Press, 1987.

760. Honeywell, Inc. *Agreement between Minneapolis Honeywell Heat Regulator Company, Minneapolis Operations, and the United Electrical, Radio and Machine Workers of America, Local 1145: Affiliated with the CIO: Relating to wages, hours and working conditions, effective September 1, 1945.* [Minneapolis, 1945]. 29 p.

761. *Humoristinen Laulukirja.* Superior: Amerikan Suomalainen Sosialistinen Kustannusliike, n.d. 123 p. In Finnish. (IHRC)
A humorous songbook.

762. *Kaikkien Työläisten, Yksi Suuri Unio IWW* (One Big Union for All Workers). Duluth: Workers Socialist Pub. Co., n.d. 31 p. In Finnish. (IHRC)
The basics of industrial unionism.

763. Karni, Michael G., ed. *For the Common Good: Finnish Immigrants and the Radical Response to Industrial America.* Superior: Työmies Society, 1977. 235 p. In Finnish. (IHRC)

764. Keillor, Steven J. *Hjalmar Petersen of Minnesota: The Politics of Provincial Independence.* St. Paul: Minnesota Historical Society Press, 1987. 342 p.

765. Kostiainen, Auvo. *The Forging of Finnish-American Communism, 1917–1924: A Study in Ethnic Radicalism.* Turku, Finland: Turun Yliopisto, 1978. 225 p.

766. Lahtinen, William, ed. *50 Vuoden Varrelta.* Superior: Työmies Society, 1953. 255 p. In Finnish.
50th anniversary history of the Työmies Society.

767. Laukki, Leo. *Teolliseen Yhteiskuntaan* (Toward an Industrial Society). Duluth: Workers Socialist Pub. Co., 1917. 568 p. In Finnish. (IHRC)
Theoretical text for the IWW.

768. Laukki, Leo. *Venäjän Vallankumous, Bolshevismi ja Soviet Tasavalta.* (The Russian Revolution, Bolshevism and the Soviet Republic). Duluth: Workers Socialist Pub. Co., 1919. 319 p. In Finnish. (IHRC)

769. Le Sueur, Meridel. *Salute to Spring.* New York: International Publisher, 1940. 191 p.

770. MacDonald, J. A. *Työttömyys ja Kone* (Unemployment and Technology). Duluth: Workers Socialist Pub. Co., 1925. 93 p. In Finnish. (IHRC)

771. Mattson, Leo. *40 Vuotta, Kuvauksia ja Muistelmia Amerikan Suomaisen Työvaënliiken Toimintataipaleelta 1906–1946.* New York: Finnish American Mutual Aid Society, 1946. 191 p. In Finnish. (IHRC)
A history of Finnish Communism in America, particularly in Minnesota and the Midwest.

772. Mayer, George H. *The Political Career of Floyd B. Olson,* Minneapolis: University of Minnesota Press, 1951; St. Paul: Minnesota Historical Society Press, Borealis Books, 1987. 329 p.

773. Mesaba Range Cooperative Park Association. *50 Years of Progressive Cooperation, 1929–1979.* Superior: The Association, 1979. 40 p.

774. Mesaba Range Cooperative Park Association. *60 Years of Progressive Cooperation, 1929–1989.* Superior: The Association, 1989. 36 p.

775. Morlan, Robert L. *Political Prairie Fire: The Nonpartisan League, 1915–1922.* Minneapolis: University of Minnesota Press, 1955; St. Paul: Minnesota Historical Society Press, Borealis Books, 1985. 414 p.

776. Murray, Robert K. *Red Scare: A Study in National Hysteria, 1919–1920.* Minneapolis: University of Minnesota Press, 1955. 337 p.

777. Neubeck, Deborah Kahn. *Guide to a Microfilm Edition of the National Nonpartisan League Papers.* St. Paul: Minnesota Historical Society, 1970. 22 p.

778. Newstrand, Emil R., ed. *Industrial, Agricultural, Labor Relations for Minnesota Living.* Minneapolis: Argus Pub. Co., 1948. 46 p.
This is a public-school manual for teaching students about these issues.

779. *Palkkaorjain Lauluja* (Songs of the Wage Slave). Duluth: Workers Socialist Pub. Co., 1925. 112 p. In Finnish. (IHRC)

780. People's Centennial Book Committee of Minnesota. *The People Together: One Hundred Years of Minnesota, 1858–1958*. Minneapolis: The Committee, 1958. 48 p.

781. Perry, Grover H. *Vallan—Kumouksellinen IWW ... Suomentanut K. Kiika* (The Revolutionary IWW ...). Duluth: Workers Socialist Pub. Co., n.d. 47 p. In Finnish. (IHRC)

782. *Proletaari Lauluja* (Songs of the Proletariat). Duluth: Workers Socialist Pub. Co., 1918. 91 p. In Finnish. (IHRC)

783. Puotinen, Arthur Edwin. *Finnish Radicals and Religion in Midwestern Mining Towns, 1865–1914*. New York: Arno Press, 1979. 339 p.

784. *Raatajain Lauluja* (Songs of the Toiler). Duluth: Workers Socialist Pub. Co., n.d. 103 p. In Finnish. (IHRC)

785. Rein, William. *Nuoriso, Oppi ja Työ* (Youth, Learning and Labor). Duluth: Workers Socialist Pub. Co., 1929. 103 p. In Finnish. (IHRC)
   IWW text.

786. Ross, Carl. *The Finn Factor in American Labor, Culture and Society*. New York Mills: Parta Printer, 1977. 220 p.

787. Ross, Carl, and K. Marianne Wargelin-Brown, eds. *Women Who Dared: The History of Finnish American Women*. St. Paul: Immigration History Research Center, University of Minnesota, 1986. 164 p.

788. Rutanen, Mikael. *Taistehin Säveliä, Lausattavia Runoja* (Melodies of Struggle, Poems for Recitation). Superior: Työmies, 1930. 93 p. In Finnish. (IHRC)

789. Rutanen, Mikael. *Unohdettujen Maailmasta (Kuvaus Metsätyöläisten elämästä)* (From the World of the Forgotten: Scenes from the Life of a Timber Worker). Superior: Amerikan Suomalaisten Sosialistinen Kustannusliike, 1929. 163 p. In Finnish. (IHRC)

790. Simler, Norman J. *The Impact of Unionism on Wage-Income Ratios in the Manufacturing Sector of the Economy*. Minneapolis: University of Minnesota Press, 1961. 71 p.

791. *Taisteleva IWW* (The Fighting IWW). Duluth: Workers Socialist Pub. Co., n.d. 31 p. In Finnish. (IHRC)

792. Two Harbors Centennial Commission. *Two Harbors 100 Years: A Pictorial History*. [Two Harbors?]: The Commission, 1983.
   Contains information on Socialist activity in Two Harbors.

793. *Two Harbors in 1910*. [Two Harbors?, 1910?]. 80 p.
   Contains information about Socialist activity in Two Harbors.

794. Työmies Society. *Lehtipaja: Tyomiehen Neljannesvuosisata Julkaisu*. Superior: The Society, 1928. 191 p. In Finnish. (IHRC)
   Twenty-fifth anniversary history of the society.

795. Työmies Society. *Seventieth Anniversary Souvenir Journal, 1903–1973*. Superior: The Society, 1973. 40 p. (IRHC)
   Seventieth anniversary history of the society.

796. Työmies Society. *Työmies Kymmenvuotias, 1903–1913, Juhlajulkaisu*. Hancock, Mich.: The Society, 1913. 160 p. In Finnish. (IHRC)

797. Työmies Society. *Työmies 20 Vuotta*. Superior: The Society, 1923. 128 p. In Finnish. (IHRC)
   Twentieth anniversary history of the society.

798. Työmies Society. *Työmies 40 Vuotta*. Superior: The Society, 1943. 32 p. In Finnish. (IHRC)
   Fortieth anniversary history of the society.

799. Työmies Society. *Työväen Laulakirja: 7-mas uusittu ja Laajennettu painos*. (The Workers Songbook, 7th Expanded Edition). Superior: Työmies Kustannusyhtio, 1915. 192 p. In Finnish. (IHRC)

800. Työmies Society. *Työväen Laulakirja: 8-mas uusittu ja Laajennettu painos*. (The Workers Songbook, 8th Expanded Edition). Superior: The Society, 1919. 189 p. In Finnish. (IHRC)

801. Työväen-Opisto [Work People's College]. *Näytelmäluettelo, 1936–37*. Duluth: Työväen-Opisto, 1937. 16 p. In Finnish. (IHRC)
   List of plays in the play library of the Work People's College.

Henning Holm, manager of the Workers Book Store in downtown Minneapolis, held a sign left by anti-Communist vigilantes who raided the store during the 1930s and burned books and pamphlets.

802. Työväen-Opisto [Work People's College]. *Suomenkielen Kielioppi, Toimittanut Työväen-Opisto.* Duluth: Työväen-Opisto, 1919. In Finnish. (IHRC)
Finnish grammar textbook.

803. United Packinghouse Workers of America. Local 9 (Austin). *Working Agreement between United Packinghouse Workers of America, Local No. 9, CIO, and Geo. A. Hormel and Company, Austin, Minnesota: As of December 6, 1940.* Austin, 1940. 39 p.

804. United States. Subversive Activities Control Board. *Official Report of Proceedings before the Subversive Activities Control Board, Hearing at Washington, D.C., January 13, 1954.* Washington, D.C.: Alderson Reporting Co., 1954. [87 p.]
Concerning Communist party activities in Minnesota. Testimony of Barbara Louise Roehrich, a party member.

805. United States Congress. House. Committee on Un-American Activities. *Communist Activities in the Minneapolis, Minn., Area.* Washington, D.C.: GPO, 1964. [258 p.]
Hearings before the committee, 88 Congress, 2d session, June 24, 25, 26, 1964, including index.

806. University of Minnesota, Minneapolis. *In the Matter of: The Investigation of Charges of Communist Affiliation Made Against Jules Chametzky and Eugene Bluestein*

by Barbara Roehrich. Proceedings, February 6, 1954. (Uarch)
Verbatim proceedings of Chametzky and Bluestein's hearing before a university investigating committee in which they disclaim any affiliation with the Communist party. They were both subsequently dismissed from positions as assistants in the English department.

807. Valelly, Richard M. *Radicalism in the States: The Minnesota Farmer-Labor Party and the American Political Economy.* Chicago: University of Chicago Press, 1989. 258 p.

808. *Vihan Vasamia* (Bolts of Hate). Duluth: Workers Socialist Pub. Co., [1919?]. 167 p. In Finnish. (IHRC)
Poems of revolutionary struggle.

809. Walker, Charles R. *The American City: A Rank and File History.* New York: Farrar and Rinehart, 1937. 278 p.
A "biography" of Minneapolis with particular emphasis on the truck drivers' strike of 1934.

810. Woodruff, Abner. *Nouseva Proletariaatti: Tutkielma Työväenliikeesta, sen Nousu Palkkaorjuudesta Vapauteen* (The Rising Proletariat: Studies in the Workers' Movement). Duluth: Työväen-Opisto, n.d. 24 p. In Finnish. (IHRC)

811. *The Young Rebel, Christmas, 1929.* Duluth: Workers Socialist Pub. Co., 1929. 32 p. In Finnish. (IHRC)

812. Youngdale, James, ed. *Third Party Footprints: An Anthology from the Writings and Speeches of Midwest Radicals.* Minneapolis: Ross and Haines, Inc., 1966. 357 p.

UNPUBLISHED PAPERS

The unpublished papers listed below are at the Minnesota Historical Society. Researchers should also visit the Immigration History Research Center and the University of Minnesota libraries to search for further dissertation titles. Many theses have been written on Minnesota history, both at the University of Minnesota and elsewhere. A useful guide is *A Bibliography of Theses on Minnesota History, Including Theses on Subjects Relating to Minnesota History, (1901–1965)* by Walter M. Ostrem (Mankato, 1966). It lists theses and also term papers, and it has a subject index. Another useful resource is *Dissertation Abstracts,* which is available at most reference libraries.

813. Asher, Hellen Drummond. "The Labor Movement in Minnesota, 1852–1890." 1925. 40 p.

814. Berman, Hyman. "Education for Work and Labor Solidarity: The Immigrant Miners and Radicalism on the Mesabi Range." 1963. 62 p. On microfilm.
    Prepared for the Conference on the Role of Education in the Minnesota Iron Range Towns, University of Minnesota, Oct. 18–19, 1963. Includes bibliographical references.

815. Blatnik, Frank P. "Culture Conflict: A Study of the Slovenes in Chisholm, Minnesota." Master's thesis, University of Minnesota, 1942. 208 p.

816. Clepper, Irene French. "Minnesota's Definition of the Sit-Down Strike: An Analysis of Union Activities in Austin, Minnesota, 1933–37, and Their Coverage by Local, State, and National Media." Ph.D. diss., University of Minnesota, 1979. 221 p.

817. Dyson, Lowell K. "The Farm Holiday Movement." Ph.D. diss., Columbia University, 1968. 283 p. On microfilm.

818. Engberg, George Barker. "The Rise of Organized Labor in Minnesota, 1850–1890." Master's thesis, University of Minnesota, 1939. 139 p.

819. Gedicks, Al (Albert Joseph). "Working Class Radicalism among Finnish Immigrants in Minnesota and Michigan Mining Communities." Ph.D. diss., University of Wisconsin–Madison, 1979. 216 p. On microfilm.

820. Halonen, Arne. "The Role of Finnish-Americans in the Political Labor Movement." Master's thesis, University of Minnesota, 1945. 149 p. On microfilm.

821. Haynes, John Earl. "Liberals, Communists, and the Popular Front in Minnesota: The Struggle to Control the Political Direction of the Labor Movement and Organized Liberalism, 1936–1950." Ph.D. diss., University of Minnesota, 1978. 889 p.

822. Kampelman, Max M. "The Communists and the C.I.O.: A Study in Political Power." Ph.D. diss., University of Minnesota, 1952. 437 p.

823. Karni, Michael G. "Yhteishyva, or, For the Common Good: Finnish Radicalism in the Western Great Lakes Region, 1900–1940." Ph.D. diss., University of Minnesota, 1975. 411 p. On microfilm.

824. Marolt, Edward. "The Development of Labor Unionism in the Iron Mining Industry of the Virginia-Eveleth District." Master's thesis, University of Minnesota, 1969. 171 p.

825. Masica, Mark Alexis. "The Albert Lea Strike: Wilson and Company vs. Freeman." Undergraduate paper, University of Minnesota, [1975?]. 83 p.

826. Naftalin, Arthur E. "A History of the Farmer-Labor Party of Minnesota." Ph.D. diss., University of Minnesota, 1948. 382 p.

827. Nord, David Paul. "Socialism in One City: A Political Study of Minneapolis in the Progressive Era." Master's thesis, University of Minnesota, 1972. 221 p.

828. Olson, Ralph C. "Robert A. Olson: Labor Leader." [Duluth?, 1971?]. 30 p.

829. Perala, Kenneth W. "The History of Logging in Selected Areas of St. Louis County." Graduate paper, University of Minnesota–Duluth, 1967. 171 p.

830. Pinola, Rudolph. "Labor and Politics on the Iron Range of Northern Minnesota." Ph.D. diss., University of Wisconsin, 1957. 232 p. On microfilm.

831. Setnicker, Norman John. "The Development of the Biwabik Mine from 1892–1920." Master's thesis, University of Minnesota, 1968. 156 p.

832. Smolen, Joseph S. "Organized Labor in Minnesota: A Brief History." [Minneapolis]: Labor Education Service, Industrial Relations Center and General Extension Division, University of Minnesota, 1964. 39 p.

833. Tselos, George Dimitri. "The Minneapolis Labor Movement in the 1930's." Ph.D. diss., University of Minnesota, 1970. 555 p. On microfilm.

ARTICLES

The periodicals listed below are available at the Minnesota Historical Society Research Center.

834. Betten, Neil. "The Origins of Ethnic Radicalism in Northern Minnesota, 1900–1920." *International Migration Review* 4 (Spring 1970): 44–56.

835. Betten, Neil. "Riot, Revolution, Repression in the Iron Range Strike of 1916." *Minnesota History* 41 (Summer 1968): 82–94.

836. Betten, Neil. "Strike on the Mesabi—1907." *Minnesota History* 40 (Fall 1967): 340–347.

837. Blantz, Thomas E. "Father Haas and the Minneapolis Truckers' Strike of 1934." *Minnesota History* 42 (Spring 1970): 5–15.

838. Choate, Jean. " ' We Want Our Money Back': The National Farmers' Process Tax Recovery Association in Minnesota." *Minnesota History* 52 (Fall 1990): 101–111.

839. Davis, Donald Derby. "No More Strikes in Minneapolis." *Review of Reviews* 93, no. 4 (1936): 32–34.

840. Dennett, Tyler. "The Mining Strike in Minnesota: The Other Side." *Outlook* 113 (Aug. 30, 1916): 1046–1048.

841. Duoos, Robert. "The Socialist in Isanti County." *Minnesota Genealogist* 6, no. 4 (1975): 9–12.

842. Engberg, George B. "Collective Bargaining in the Lumber Industry of the Upper Great Lakes States." *Agricultural History* 24 (1950): 205–211.

843. Engberg, George B. "The Knights of Labor in Minnesota." *Minnesota History* 22 (Dec. 1941): 367–390.

844. Engberg, George B. "The Rise of Organized Labor in Minnesota." *Minnesota History* 21 (Dec. 1940): 372–394.

845. Erickson, Herman. "WPA Strike and Trial of 1939." *Minnesota History* 42 (Summer 1971): 203–214.

846. Field, Ben. "The First Red Mayor." *New Masses* 9 (Sept. 1933): 22–23.

847. Harter, Clarence. "The Necessary Struggle." *Northern Oratorical League*, 1908, p. 18–22.

848. Hain, A. J. "Twin Cities Team for Open Shop." *Iron Trade Review* 68 (Mar. 17, 1921): 762–768.

849. Haynes, John Earl. " *The New Times:* A Frustrated Voice of Socialism, 1910–1919." *Minnesota History* 52 (Spring 1991): 183–194.

850. Haynes, John Earl. "Revolt of the 'Timber Beasts': IWW Lumber Strike in Minnesota." *Minnesota History* 42 (Spring 1971): 162–174.

851. Henry, Ralph Chester [Erik Thane, pseud.]. "The 'Red Menace' in Minnesota." *Nation* 139 (1934): 435–436.

852. Hudson, Carlos N. "Minneapolis—One Year Later." *Nation* 141 (1935): 512–514.

853. Hyman, Colette. "Culture as Strategy: Popular Front Politics and the Minneapolis Theatre Union, 1935–39." *Minnesota History* 52 (Winter 1991): 294–306.

854. Jenson, Carol. "Loyalty as a Political Weapon: The 1918 Campaign in Minnesota." *Minnesota History* 43 (Summer 1972): 43–57.

855. Karni, Michael Gary. "The Founding of the Finnish Socialist Federation and the Minnesota Strike of 1907." Superior: Tyomies Society, [1977?]. [21 p.] Reprinted from *For the Common Good: Finnish Immigrants and the Radical Response to Industrial America.* Superior: Tyomies Society, 1977, p. 65–86.

856. Kelly, Fred C. "You Bet Your Life I'm a Radical!" *Today* 3 (Dec. 22/29, 1934): 8–9.

857. Knuuti, Rosa. "The Work Peoples' College." *Industrial Pioneer*, Oct. 1921, p. 59–61.

858. Le Sueur, Meridel. "What Happens in a Strike." *American Mercury* 33, no. 131 (1934): 329–335.

An account of the truck drivers' strikes in Minneapolis, May 15–26, July 17–Aug. 22, 1934.

859. Lovoll, Odd S. "*Gaa Paa*: A Scandinavian Voice of Dissent." *Minnesota History* 52 (Fall 1990): 90–99.

860. MacDonald, Dwight. "WPA Cuts—or Jail." *Nation* 150 (1940): 120–123.

861. Millikan, William. "Defenders of Business: The Minneapolis Civic and Commerce Association *Versus* Labor During W.W.I." *Minnesota History* 50 (Spring 1986): 2–17.

862. Millikan, William. "Maintaining Law and Order: The Minneapolis Citizens Alliance in the 1920s." *Minnesota History* 51 (Summer 1989): 219–233.

863. Mindak, William A. "Economic Effects of the Minneapolis Newspaper Strike." *Journalism Quarterly* 40, no. 2 (1963): 213–218.

864. Mitau, G. Theodore. "The Democratic-Farmer-Labor Party Schism of 1948." *Minnesota History* 34 (Spring 1955): 187–194.

865. Morlan, Robert L. "The Nonpartisan League and the Minnesota Campaign of 1918." *Minnesota History* 34 (Summer 1955): 221–232.

866. Nielson, Kim. "Who Were These Farmer Radicals? The Douglas County Farm Holiday Association." *Minnesota History* 51 (Fall 1989): 270–285.

867. Nord, David Paul. "Minneapolis and the Pragmatic Socialism of Thomas Van Lear." *Minnesota History* 45 (Spring 1976): 3–10.

868. Pahl, Thomas L. "G-string Conspiracy: Political Reprisal or Armed Revolt?: The Minneapolis Trotskyites Trial." *Labor History* 8 (1967): 30–51.

869. Pruitt, Mary C. " 'Lady Organizer': Sabrie G. Akin and the *Labor World*." *Minnesota History* 52 (Summer 1991): 206–219.

870. Quam, Lois, and Peter Rachleff. "Keeping Minneapolis an Open-Shop Town: The Citizens Alliance in the 1930s." *Minnesota History* 50 (Fall 1986): 105–117.

871. Ross, Carl. "How Far We Have Come: A Report on the 20th-Century Radicalism in Minnesota Project." *Minnesota History* 51 (Winter 1988): 138–144.

872. Shover, John L. "The Communist Party and the Midwest Farm Crisis of 1933." *Journal of American History* 51 (1964): 248–266.

873. Smith, Vera. "Work Peoples' College." *One Big Union Monthly*, Apr. 1938, p. 14–15.

874. Sofchalk, Donald G. "Organized Labor and the Iron Ore Miners of Northern Minnesota, 1907–1936." *Labor History* 12 (Spring 1971): 214–242.

875. Solow, Herbert. "War in Minneapolis." *Nation* 139 (1934): 160–161.

876. Starr, Karen. "Fighting for a Future: Farm Women of the Nonpartisan League." *Minnesota History* 48 (Summer 1983): 255–262.

877. Stuhler, Barbara. "The One Man Who Voted 'Nay': The Story of John T. Bernard's Quarrel with American Foreign Policy, 1937–38." *Minnesota History* 43 (Fall 1972): 83–92.

878. Thompson, Fred. "School Days at Work Peoples' College." *One Big Union Monthly*, Apr. 1938, p. 18–20.

879. Vorse, Mary Heaton. "The Mining Strike in Minnesota: From the Miners' Point of View." *Outlook* 113 (Aug. 30, 1916): 1036–1046.

880. Walker, Charles Rumford. "The Farmer-Labor Party in Minnesota." *Nation* 144 (1937): 292–294, 318–320.

881. Walker, Charles Rumford. "Minneapolis . . ." *Survey Graphic* 25 (1936): 549–555, 584–589, 620–623, 633–634; 26 (1937): 26–33.

882. Walljasper, Jay. "A Striking Victory." *Minneapolis/St. Paul* 10 (Aug. 1982): 87–89.

883. Wefald, Jon M. "Congressman Knud Wefald: A Minnesota Voice for Farm Parity." *Minnesota History* 38 (Dec. 1962): 177–185.

Selected Works on National and International Radical Activity

An examination of national and international aspects of radical activity puts Minnesota radicalism in a broader context. Some national and international materials are available at the Minnesota Historical Society; however, the libraries at the University of Minnesota and the collections at the Immigration History Research Center offer a more complete collection of primary and secondary materials.

UNIVERSITY OF MINNESOTA LIBRARIES: SELECTED RESOURCES ON RADICALISM

Most of the materials at the University of Minnesota in Minneapolis are accessible via LUMINA, the university libraries' computerized catalog, by author, title, key words, or subject. There are, however, certain categories of materials, such as journal articles and some special collections, that are not on LUMINA. Where appropriate, this will be noted in the information that follows.

Wilson Library on the West Bank campus houses the main social sciences and humanities collections, which include most of the materials concerning radicalism. An open stack arrangement is used. Some older materials, however, are in the closed stacks at either Wilson Library or Walter Library on the university's East Bank campus. These items are not readily available, but staff will page items during certain hours.

The general university collection contains many pamphlets and books published by radical and antiradical presses and purchased by the university in the 19th and early 20th centuries. These items are easily accessed on LUMINA and are stored in the open stacks. They include works by Norman M. Thomas, Daniel DeLeon, Eugene V. Debs, William Z. Foster, Earl Browder, and other radical leaders and thinkers, as well as campaign and single-issue pamphlets. Also available is a wide selection of anti-Communist publications. Some of these publications are part of the Pamphlet Collec-

tion at Wilson Library. The Pamphlet Collection is poorly organized for browsing, but most of its titles are on LUMINA, and a librarian can provide further assistance. Pamphlets are also found in the microfilm collections (described below). In addition to the general collection, the libraries hold other important sources (discussed below) for researching radicalism.

Microform Research Collections

Large collections of primary source materials have been filmed by commercial microfilm corporations. The microfilm is available at the university libraries. All of these microfilm collections have a reference guide or index (unless otherwise noted). These guides are cited on LUMINA. Individual items within the microfilm collections are not cited on LUMINA.

884. American Civil Liberties Union. *Records and Publications, 1917–1975*. Glen Rock, N.J.: Microfilming Corp. of America, 1976.

885. Browder, Earl. *Earl Browder Papers, 1891–1975*. Glen Rock, N.J.: Microfilming Corp. of America, 1976.

886. Congress of Racial Equality. *The Papers of the Congress of Racial Equality, 1941–1967*. Sanford, N.C.: Microfilming Corp. of America, 1980.

887. *J. Robert Oppenheimer: FBI Security File*. Wilmington, Del.: Scholarly Resources, 1978. No guide available.

888. *Marcus Garvey: FBI Investigation File*. Wilmington, Del.: Scholarly Resources, 1978. No guide available.

889. National Woman's Party. *National Woman's Party Papers, 1913–1974*. Glen Rock, N.J.: Microfilming Corp. of America, 1977–78.

890. Rosenberg, Julius (1918–53), Defendant. *U.S. v. Rosenberg.* Conspiracy Trials in America, 1919–1953. Prepared by the Fund for the Republic. Wilmington, Del.: M. Glazier, 1978. No index available.

891. Socialist Party (U.S.). *Socialist Party of America Papers, 1897–1963.* Glen Rock, N.J.: Microfilming Corp. of America, 1975.

892. Socialist Party (U.S.). *Socialist Party of America Papers, Addendum 1919–1976.* Sanford, N.C.: Microfilming Corp. of America, 1979.

893. United States. Commission on Industrial Relations. *U.S. Commission on Industrial Relations, 1912–1915: Unpublished Records of the Division of Research and Investigation: Reports, Staff Studies, and Background Research Materials.* Frederick, Md.: University Publications of America, 1985.

894. United States. Immigrant Commission, 1907–10. *Reports.* Washington, D.C.: GPO, 1911. No index available.

895. United States. President's Mediation Commission. *The President's Mediation Committee, 1917–1918.* Frederick, Md.: University Publications of America, 1985.

896. *U.S. Military Intelligence Reports: Surveillance of Radicals in the United States, 1917–1941.* Frederick, Md.: University Publications of America, 1984.

Newspapers

The university libraries carry most major United States and some non-United States newspapers. The libraries also have a substantial collection of national radical newspapers (for Minnesota newspapers, see Chapter 2). Newspapers at the university are not listed on LUMINA; however, they are cataloged and accessible through the card file in the Newspapers/Periodicals Collection in Wilson Library.

897. *American Freeman.* Girard, Kans., 1948–49.

898. *Commonwealth.* Sarasota, Fla.: League for Group Democracy and Government by Civic Council, 1935–36.

899. *Conscientious Objector.* New York, 1937–46.

900. *Daily Worker.* New York, 1924–58.

901. *Fighting Worker.* Chicago: Revolutionary League of the United States, 1940–47.

902. *Industrial Worker.* Chicago: Industrial Workers of the World, 1910–45.

903. *Labor Action.* New York: Workers Party Section of the Fourth International, 1940–58.

904. *Militant.* New York: Communist League of America, 1928–34.

905. *Militant.* New York: Socialist Party of New York, Left Wing Branch, 1937–present.

906. *New Militant.* New York, 1934–36.

907. *People's Press.* Chicago, 1936–38.

908. *Progressive.* Madison, Wis., 1930–47.

909. *Socialist Call.* New York: Socialist Party, 1942–52.

910. *Toiler.* New York, 1919–22.

911. *United Mine Workers Journal.* Indianapolis, 1917–67.

912. *Weekly People.* New York: Socialist Labor Party, 1932, 1937–58.

913. *Weekly Review.* New York: Young Communist League, U.S.A., 1936–43.

914. *Woman's Journal.* Boston: National American Woman Suffrage Assn., 1893–1917.

915. *Worker.* New York, 1936–61.
    Sunday edition of *Daily Worker.*

916. *Worker.* New York, 1936–68. (Note: The holdings are incomplete)

917. *Worker's Challenge.* New York, 1922.

Periodicals

The university libraries collected many radical periodicals upon publication. In addition, the university has obtained periodicals from the reprint set, *Radical Periodicals in the United States, 1890–1950,* to complete this substantial collection of radical journals. Periodicals are on LUMINA and are located in the Newspapers/Periodicals Collection in Wilson Library, with the exception of a few titles, whose locations are noted on LUMINA. Some detailed bibliographies, listed below, are also available.

918. Conlin, Joseph R., ed. *The America Radical Press, 1880–1960.* Westport, Conn.: Greenwood Press, 1974.

919. Daniel, Walter C. *Black Journals of the United States.* Westport, Conn.: Greenwood Press, 1982.

920. Naas, Bernard G. *American Labor Union Periodicals, A Guide to Their Location.* Ithaca: Cornell University Press, 1956.

921. Skidmore, Gail, and Theodore Jurgen Spahn. *From Radical Left to Extreme Right.* Metuchen, N.J.: Scarecrow Press, 1987.

Periodicals are also good sources of secondary materials. Research published in scholarly journals can be accessed through a variety of indexes. Two especially useful indexes for research on radicalism are *America: History and Life* and *Historical Abstracts.*

Theses

Many theses have been written on Minnesota history, both at the University of Minnesota and elsewhere. A useful guide is *A Bibliography of Theses on Minnesota History, including Theses on Subjects Relating to Minnesota History, (1901–1965)* by Walter Ostrem (Mankato, 1966). It lists theses and also term papers, and it has a subject index. When the university library obtains theses written elsewhere, they are cataloged as any other item. University of Minnesota theses are handled differently. Master's theses and doctoral dissertations cataloged prior to 1973 are accessible through LUMINA by author, title, and subject. Doctoral dissertations since 1973 have been given only author and title access, since subject coverage is provided in *Dissertation Abstracts.*

Special Collection

The Tell G. Dahllöf Collection of Swedish-Americana contains a group of Socialist pamphlets from the late 19th and early 20th centuries. Although the scope is national, there are items documenting Minnesota activities, such as speeches delivered in the area and local publishing activities. Most items are in Swedish, including some interesting Swedish translations of Marx, Engels, and DeLeon published in Minneapolis. This collection is not accessible through LUMINA.

Government Publications Library

Government publications are rich sources of information on any subject in which the government is involved. If a government body investigates a subject or an organization, authorizes or funds a program, or regulates an agency or activity, a record of that activity can be found in its publications. In addition, the government collects a variety of statistics that are useful in research. The Government Publications Library at the university contains a fairly complete collection of federal and state publications. Most of these materials are not on LUMINA. However, they are indexed in a variety of specialized guides that are kept in the Government Publications Library. Three main government resources that are especially pertinent to the study of radicalism in Minnesota are the publications of the U.S. Congress and the Minnesota state agencies and the records from the federal decennial censuses.

The hearings, documents, and reports of the U.S. Congress contain detailed information on various aspects of radicalism in the United States, including investigations of specific organizations and activities in states and cities. To find documents published before 1970, the *CIS US Congressional Committee Hearings Index* and the *CIS US Serial Set Index* are essential. Special indexes also cover collections of unpublished hearings from the U.S. House and Senate. The researcher can search the indexes by personal and organization names, places, and specific events. The following are examples of some of the subject headings used in these indexes: Anarchists, Communism, Congressional investigations, Farmer-Labor Association of Minnesota, Labor disputes, Minnesota Farmers Union.

Among the major publications that can be found through these indexes are the publications of the U.S. House Un-American Activities Committee, which con-

A few women and a child joined the mostly male First District of the Scandinavian Socialist party members who gathered in Duluth on Labor Day weekend, 1915.

tain many references to Minnesota individuals and organizations. The *Investigation of Un-American Propaganda Activities in the U.S.* (17 volumes), for instance, includes an investigation into the Communist influences in Minnesota farmer-labor organizations. Minnesotans who testified can also be located by name in the *CIS Hearings Index.* The *Cumulative Index to Publications of the Committee on Un-America Activities, 1938–1954* has separate indexes for individuals, publications, and organizations.

Publications of the U.S. Census Bureau are helpful in researching the ethnic composition of Minnesota communities. The decennial censuses contain data such as country of birth, parents' country of birth, citizenship, language, and year of immigration, which are useful in determining the make-up of communities and are available at the city, village, and township level. Labor force and occupation statistics are also included, sometimes with nativity data, but generally only at the county or city level. The actual census records provide still more detail, including the above information for each census return. These are available on microfilm for the years 1900, 1910, and 1920.

The annual reports of such Minnesota state agencies as the Department of Labor, the Railroad and Warehouse Commission, and the Industrial Commission

may contain reports or statistics that shed light on labor-related issues. There are no comprehensive subject indexes, but research may proceed from a known agency or known time period.

Election returns for federal and state offices are found in the *Legislative Manuals.* These volumes report votes down to the township, village, and ward level and can be used with census data to compare the political compositions of communities with particular ethnic backgrounds.

IMMIGRATION HISTORY RESEARCH CENTER

The Immigration History Research Center (IHRC) of the University of Minnesota is a national library and archives established in 1965 for the purpose of collecting the records of American immigrant and ethnic groups. The holdings reflect the "new immigration" that came to America after 1880 from Eastern, Central, and Southern Europe and the Mideast.

Because the majority of these immigrants became industrial workers, the IHRC's more than two dozen ethnic collections contain substantial resource materials on working-class and labor history. The Finnish, Italian, and South Slav collections, in particular, provide a rich source of documentation on the mobilization of immigrants into the labor and socialist movements. Items in the Finnish collection are especially pertinent to Minnesota radicalism and have been included in this bibliography. Also part of the collection is one box of Carl Ross's papers.

In addition to the archival collections, the IHRC holds complete files of many radical and labor serials and newspapers. Some of the best documentation of radical activity can be found in the non-English-language, working-class press. Radical serials and newspapers are a particular strength of the IHRC's Italian collection, which includes substantial files of titles like *L'Adunatat dei Refraatari* (The Gathering of the Refractories),

1922–71, *La Parola del Socialisti* (The Word of the Socialists), 1908–present, and *Il Proletario* (The Proletarian), 1899–1946. The Slovene collection contains significant ethnic labor papers, such as *Proletarec* (The Proletarian), 1906–52, and *Glas Naroda* (The Voice of the Nation), 1893–1954. The IHRC holds all of the major Finnish-American newspapers. In addition to those titles published in the Duluth-Superior area (see Chapter 2), the collection also holds titles like the *Raivaaja* (Pioneer), 1905–present, of Fitchburg, Mass., *Toveri* (Comrade), 1921, 1926, of Astoria, Oreg., and the rare Estonian-American *Uus Ilm*, 1912–30, a Socialist, later Communist, weekly.

Index

Abraham Lincoln Brigade, 316, 329; insignia, 703
Action (Minneapolis), periodical, 521, 705
Adams, Elmer Ellsworth, papers, 456
AFL, *see* American Federation of Labor
AFL-CIO, 491; leaders, 387, 609; periodical, 726
African Americans, 369; in unions, 327, 361, 364, 388; community life, 347, 357, 358; periodicals, 919; speakers, *8*
Agricultural National Industrial Union, 694
Agricultural Workers Industrial Union, publication, 78
Agriculture, newspaper coverage, 251, 278, 282, 284, 288; farmers' rally, 296; organizations, 301, 505, 513, 569; protest movements, 328, 329, 349, 350, 688, 689, 838; depression, 403, 495; farm-labor conflicts, 427; farm life, 436, 439; conditions, 492, 638; cooperatives, 500, 584, 621; strikes, 612; collective bargaining, 669; educational materials, 778; role of Communists, 872
Ahjo (The Forge) (Duluth), periodical, 706
Ahlteen, Carl, editor, 226, 229
Akin, Sabrie G., newspaper founder, 260, 869
Albert Lea, strike, 390, 441, 645, 825
Albert Lea Freeborn Patriot, newspaper, 277
Albinson, Sophie, editor, 721
Aley, H. S., author, 14
All American Society, Minneapolis, periodical, 728
Allarm (Minneapolis), newspaper, 226; editor, 312; discussed, *ix*
Allen, Albert V., interview, 358
Amalgamated Association of Street Electric Railway and Motor Coach Employees of America, Local *1005*, 354, 700
Amalgamated Clothing Workers of America International, 386; Twin Cities Joint Board, 457
Amalgamated Meat Cutters' Union, 116
Amerasia, magazine, 683

America First (St. Paul), periodical, 707
America First Assn., 603; correspondence, 456; papers, 458
America First party, ideology, 206
American Anti-Communist Assn., 125
American Anti-Socialist League, Minneapolis, 51
American Bolshevik (Minneapolis), 227
American Civil Liberties Union, correspondence, 569; records, 884
American Committee for Protection of the Foreign Born, 315, 370, 504
American Committee of Minneapolis, publications, 25, 28, 29, 32, 38–42, 4–49, 58–60, 67
American Commonwealth Political Federation, 506, 677; correspondence, 572
American Constitution (Minneapolis), newspaper, 254
American Consumers Union, investigates strikes, 559
American Cooperative Alliance, 529
American Express, legal cases, 584
American Federation of Labor (AFL), supports Communists, 97; unions, 116, 309, 457, 502; newspaper coverage, 254, 260, 262, 265, 268; newspapers, 266, 271; relations with CIO, 259, 263, 341; merger with CIO, 298, 384, 441; split with CIO, 392; correspondence, 459, 484; organizers, 527, 532, 649, 667
American Federation of State, County, and Municipal Employees, 598
American Freeman (Girard, Kans.), newspaper, 897
American Guardian, newspaper, 288
American League for a Free Palestine, 677
American Legion, newspaper coverage, 271
American Library Assn., 470
American News, columnist, 568
American Security Alliance Organization, 477
American Student Union, members, 344
American Veterans Committee, activities, 319

American Youth Congress, members, 344; leaders, 348
American Youth for Democracy, leaders, 348, 629
Americanism Bulletin (Faribault), periodical, 708
Americanization, correspondence, 484, 528; loyalty issues, 580; on iron range, 607, 651
Americans for Democratic Action, 211, 521, 572, 581
Amerikan Suomalaisten Sosialististen Kuustannusliikke, (Hancock, Mich., and Superior), publisher, 737
Amidon, Paul, supporters, 462
Anarchism, discussed, 15, 670
Anderson, Eugenie Moore, papers, 460
Anderson, Jacob, interviews, 296, 367
Anderson, Juls J., editor, 247
Anderson, William, 565; compiler, 461
Andrew Schoch Grocery, St. Paul, strike, 582
Anti-Compulsory Military Drill League, University of Minnesota, papers, 463
Antilla, Anton, interview, 368
Anti-Socialist League, investigating committee, 518
Anvil, The (New York), periodical, 731
Appeal to Reason (Minneapolis), periodical, 709
Arbeidsmanden (The Worker) (Fertile and Crookston), newspaper, 255
Armour Co., union, 168
Arness, Ole J., legal case, 484
Arnio, Arnold F., interview, 297
Art and artists, federal projects, 300, 353, 356, 476
Artists' Union, activities, 317, 353
Asher, Hellen Drummond, author, 813
Aufderheide, Herman, papers, 464
Austin, Isabel, letters, 538
Austin, strike, 385, 390, 437, 449, 816; union, 803

Bakken, J. P., editor, 255
Ball, Joseph Hurst, papers, 465; candidate, 471
Ball, W. R., teacher, 562
Bang, Gustav, author, 11, 15

INDEX

INDEX

PICTURE CREDITS